YELLOWSTONE

The Official Guide to Touring America's First National Park

YELLOWSTONE
ASSOCIATION

CONTENTS

CONTENTS

©1997 The Yellowstone Association. Updated 1998.

All rights reserved, including the right to reproduce this book or parts thereof in any form, except for inclusion of brief quotations in a review.

Published by The Yellowstone Association. Pat Cole, Executive Director; Debbie Thomas, Project Coordinator.

Design, typesetting, and other prepress work by Falcon Press® Publishing Co., Inc., Helena, MT.

ISBN 0-934948-03-8

Library of Congress Catalog Card Number: 97-60832

Front Cover Photo: Michael Sample

Back Cover Photo: Carol Polich

Printed in U.S.A. on recycled paper.

All wildlife photographs in this book were taken from a distance using telephoto lenses. All photographs are of free-roaming animals.

   This symbol is found throughout this book where self-guiding trails are described. Leaflets to guide you on these trails can be found at the trailheads and at visitor centers.

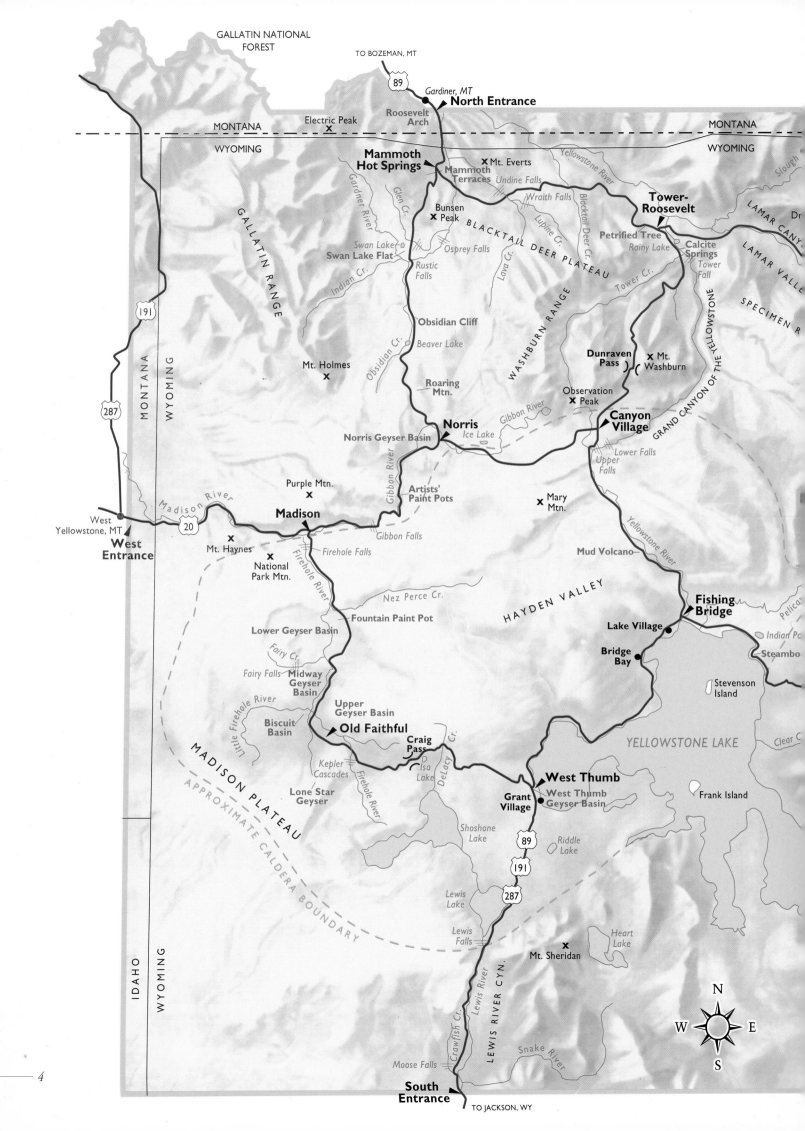

GALLATIN NATIONAL FOREST

TO BOZEMAN, MT

89

Gardiner, MT

North Entrance

MONTANA

Electric Peak ✕

Roosevelt Arch

WYOMING

Mammoth Hot Springs

✕ Mt. Everts

Mammoth Terraces

Undine Falls

Wraith Falls

Yellowstone River

MONTANA

WYOMING

Tower-Roosevelt

GALLATIN RANGE

Gardner River

Glen Cr.

Bunsen ✕ Peak

BLACKTAIL DEER PLATEAU

Lupine Cr.

Blacktail Deer Cr.

Rainy Lake

Petrified Tree

Calcite Springs

Tower Fall

LAMAR CANYON

Dr

Swan Lake o

Osprey Falls

Swan Lake Flat

Rustic Falls

Lava Cr.

WASHBURN RANGE

Tower Cr.

LAMAR VALLEY

SPECIMEN R.

191

Indian Cr.

Obsidian Cr.

Obsidian Cliff

Beaver Lake

287

Mt. Holmes ✕

Roaring Mtn.

Dunraven Pass) ✕ Mt. Washburn

Observation ✕ Peak

GRAND CANYON OF THE YELLOWSTONE

Gibbon River

Norris

Ice Lake

Canyon Village

Norris Geyser Basin

Lower Falls

Upper Falls

Purple Mtn. ✕

Artists' Paint Pots

✕ Mary Mtn.

Madison River

West Yellowstone, MT

20

Madison

Gibbon Falls

Mud Volcano

Yellowstone River

West Entrance

Mt. Haynes ✕

Firehole Falls

✕ National Park Mtn.

Firehole River

Nez Perce Cr.

HAYDEN VALLEY

Fishing Bridge

Fountain Paint Pot

Lower Geyser Basin

Fairy Cr.

Lake Village ●

Fairy Falls

Midway Geyser Basin

Little Firehole River

Biscuit Basin

Upper Geyser Basin

Old Faithful

Craig Pass

Kepler Cascades

Lone Star Geyser

Firehole River

DeLacy Cr.

Isa Lake

Bridge Bay ●

Stevenson Island

YELLOWSTONE LAKE

Clear C

Indian Po

Steambo

MADISON PLATEAU

APPROXIMATE CALDERA BOUNDARY

Shoshone Lake

West Thumb

Grant Village

West Thumb Geyser Basin

Frank Island

89

191

287

Riddle Lake

Lewis Lake

IDAHO

WYOMING

Lewis Falls

Heart Lake

Mt. Sheridan ✕

LEWIS RIVER CYN.

Crawfish Cr.

Lewis River

Snake River

N

W   E

S

Moose Falls

South Entrance

TO JACKSON, WY

YELLOWSTONE

YELLOWSTONE NATIONAL PARK

TO COOKE
CITY, MT

Baronnette
Peak **x**

Northeast Entrance

x
Abiathar
Peak

x The Thunderer

12

x
Mt. Norris

Soda Butte Cr.

Pebble Cr.

Lamar River

ABSAROKA RANGE

Legend

➤	**Entrance or Road Segment Origin**
) (	**Pass**
—	Area of Interest
x	Mountain Peak
●	**Additional Visitor Services Area**
🝆	*Lakes*
～	*Rivers, Creeks*
╫	*Waterfalls*
━	**U.S. Highway**
– – –	**45th Parallel**
▬	**Park Boundary**

0   5 km   10   Kilometers

0   5 mi   10   Miles

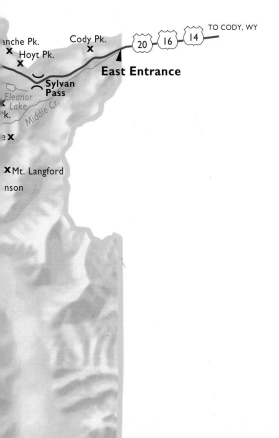

anche Pk.
x   Cody Pk.
Hoyt Pk. **x**   **x**

20 16 14   TO CODY, WY

East Entrance

**Sylvan
Pass**

*Eleanor
Lake*

Middle Cr.

e **x**

x Mt. Langford

nson

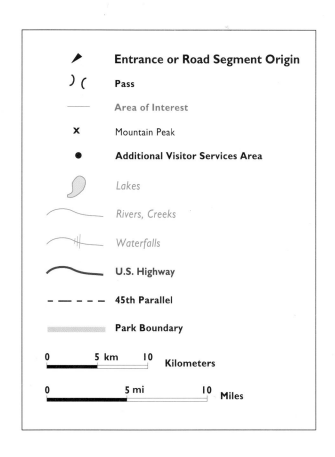

5

Introduction

*O*f the few untrammeled places still left to us to protect, it would be hard to think of any that ignite the imagination more quickly, more surely, than Yellowstone National Park. Those who come seeking glimpses of the dramatic have no trouble finding it here: in the sizzle and gush of the thermal basins, or the headlong plunge of Upper Yellowstone Falls; in the startling colors of Grand Prismatic Spring, or the bizarre sculpting of Excelsior and Grotto Geysers. Indeed, there are times when even the plants of Yellowstone can be startling; great sweeps of fireweed wash the floors of burned forests in blankets of lavender, while in autumn, aspen leaves in the draws above the Lamar River glow so brightly in the October sun that they seem lit from within. So, too, is this a place of plenty for those who celebrate nature with their ears—the piercing bugle of elk ringing through the hills near Mammoth, the plop and gurgle of mud pots along Pelican Creek, the yip of coyotes, and the soft thunder of bison hooves pounding across Hayden Valley.

As if that were not enough, underlying all these natural delights is the sheer significance of Yellowstone, the world's very first national park. The power of Yellowstone's legacy is that it emphasizes what it means to be good stewards of the land. Somehow our visits here leave us feeling a little more generous, a little more willing to speak for the magic that yet lies in the last of the wild places.

This guidebook was written with two goals in mind. First, we want to give you the basics—the what, when, and where of Yellowstone. We hope to help you experience a safe, fun, and hassle-free visit and to send you on your way armed with the ingredients for a truly memorable journey. Beyond that, the pages that follow will also serve as an introduction to some of the most extraordinary threads in the park's natural

Above right: The Lamar River winds peacefully through its namesake valley. MICHAEL SAMPLE

Facing page: The Grand Canyon of the Yellowstone River is roughly 23 miles long and at its deepest point is 1,200 feet deep. Magnificent Lower Falls is the park's highest waterfall at 308 feet. MICHAEL SAMPLE

and cultural history, as well as many of the recreational opportunities waiting for you along Yellowstone's primary roadways.

As you can see from the map on page 4, the road system consists of two large loops lying back to back. These loops are located in the central and north-central parts of the park, forming roughly the shape of a figure 8. From the loops, spur roads extend like spokes on the hub of a wheel—two heading east, one south, one west, and a short spur heading north from park headquarters at Mammoth Hot Springs. This book guides you along these routes section by section, from one major attraction to another, enabling you to explore Yellowstone in individual segments.

In addition to the map of the entire park, there are smaller detail maps at the beginning of each road section description. Visitor centers, lodging, campgrounds, and other services are included on these maps, as are a variety of walks and hikes, perfect for those who long to get away from the road system. We have also included in each section the location of self-guiding trails, for which informative trail leaflets are available at trailheads and at visitor centers. In general, these self-guiding trails are designed to help you explore areas of interest where potential hazards may exist. It is a good idea to pick up the leaflets and study any safety information contained within.

Finally, on page 72 you will find a field guide to help you identify and learn about Yellowstone's wide variety of birds, plants, and mammals. ⤳

Monkeyflower blooms cradle a hot springs runoff channel in the Lower Geyser Basin. The relatively mild winter temperatures found in thermal basins allow many plants to thrive, which in turn encourages wildlife to feed there.

JEFF FOOTT

Bison at Black Sand Basin. This area, which lies just west of Old Faithful, takes its name from the small chips of obsidian that make up a portion of the sand near here. People passing by can spook animals, causing them to run and perhaps scald themselves in the springs. While you should always keep your distance from Yellowstone's wildlife, be especially careful in thermal areas.

MICHAEL SAMPLE

Yellowstone by Road and Trail

*B*efore you begin your tour of Yellowstone, orient yourself. How much time do you have to spend in the park, and how would you like to use it: Watching eruptions in the geyser basins? Looking for wildlife? Hiking the Grand Canyon of the Yellowstone River? Maybe walking to the summit of Mount Washburn? Visitors often find it helpful to make a list of all the things they really want to do, taking their best guess at how long their explorations might take. If you find yourself short on days, make some priorities. Besides studying the information and maps in this guidebook, when you enter the park be sure to study *Yellowstone Today*, the newspaper you will receive at the entrance gate. In the newspaper, you will find a wealth of helpful information: updates on road conditions and construction, news about special events and interpretive programs, and park regulations. Stopping by the visitor center or Yellowstone Association bookstore at each major location will also be helpful. Yellowstone is an enormous place. The hour or two you spend right now thinking about what to see and how to get there will save you time and frustration in the long run.

Take a few minutes to read the following sections describing the natural and cultural history that make Yellowstone such a unique, engaging place. Of course we cannot tell the whole story of how this place came to be. That would take volumes! But even a little knowledge about Yellowstone will help you unlock a great many of the mysteries waiting for you around the next corner. ☙

Yellowstone Geology

*M*ost of us tend to think of geology as a slow, tedious process—nips and tucks made to the earth over spans of time too extensive to even comprehend—the grind of glaciers, and mountains rising over millions of years, then quietly being worn down again over millions more by rain, ice, and wind. But another, much different kind of geology is going on in many parts of Yellowstone, a shocking kind of earth drama marked by rapid changes in the shapes and colors of things, changes you can easily track over weeks or months, or sometimes in an instant. If you have not already guessed, we are talking about Yellowstone's geothermal areas. In these areas, water from rain or snowmelt seeps down through cracks in the Earth's crust. The water is then superheated by a chamber of partially molten rock (magma) that lies just a few miles under the surface. This enormous magma chamber, thought to be hundreds of miles deep, heats the water, causing it to rise again in a wonderful display of bubbling, spouting water, steam, and mud. It is this unique combination of water flowing very near a pocket of hot magma that gives Yellowstone its geologic magic. You will get a better feel for these processes when you visit places like the Mammoth Terraces, Old Faithful, and the Norris Geyser Basin. The park contains more geysers than all the rest of the Earth combined.

The magma chamber described above has done a lot more for Yellowstone's landscape than simply heat the water. Over time, heat from this magma not only melted the lower layers of the Earth's crust, but pushed it upward with tremendous pressure, stretching and thinning it. Some 650,000 years ago, this pressure became so great that the chamber exploded with terrific force, spewing volcanic ash as far away as Kansas and Nebraska. As all this material emptied out of the chamber, the crust that rested on top of it collapsed, creating a volcanic crater. Scientists call this crater a caldera. The Yellowstone Caldera—the rims of which you will be driving over—is one of the largest in the world.

One last, widely held geologic theory worth mentioning is a process called plate tectonics. According to this theory, the Earth's crust is broken into sections, or plates, overlapping one another as they drift over the underlying layer of hot plastic rock known as the Earth's mantle. The large plate that includes the Yellowstone area is sliding southwest. What all of this means is that sometime in the distant future, an entirely different section of earth, probably land near the Beartooth Mountains around Cooke City, Montana, will drift over the big magma chamber currently under the park. If pressures inside the Earth are sufficient, this new cover may then undergo an enormous volcanic explosion of its own, afterward collapsing to form yet another caldera. ༄

A

B

C
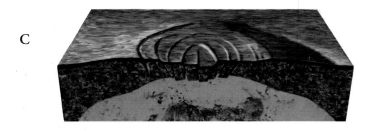

D

These four schematic diagrams show the idealized stages in the development of the Yellowstone caldera 650,000 years ago.

Fig. A: *A large magma chamber formed deep within the Earth, and the molten rock began to force its way slowly toward the surface. As it pushed upward, it arched the overlying rocks in a broad dome. The arching produced a series of concentric fractures, or a ring fracture zone, around the crest of the dome. The fractures extended downward toward the top of the magma chamber.*

Fig. B: *The ring fractures eventually tapped the magma chamber, the uppermost part of which contained a high proportion of dissolved gases. With the sudden release of pressure, tremendous amounts of hot gases and molten rock were erupted almost instantly. The liquid solidified into pumice, ash, and dust as it was blown out. Some of the dust and ash was blown high into the air and carried along by the wind, but much of the debris moved outward across the landscape as vast ash flows, covering thousands of square miles very rapidly.*

Fig. C: *The area overlying the blown-out part of the magma chamber collapsed to form a gigantic caldera. The collapse took place mostly along normal faults that developed from the fractures in the ring fracture zone. The depth of the collapse was probably several thousand feet.*

Fig. D: *Renewed rise of molten rock domed the caldera floor above the magma chamber. A series of rhyolite lava flows poured out through fractures in the surrounding ring fracture zone and spread across the caldera floor.*

Reprinted from *Recent and Ongoing Geology of Grand Teton and Yellowstone National Parks* by John M. Good and Kennth L. Pierce. Copyright 1996 by the Grand Teton Natural History Association.

Illustrations by Lawrence Ormsby after W. R. Keefer, 1971
USGS Bulletin 1347, p. 40.

Human History

*D*iscoveries made by archaeologists suggest humans were probably using parts of what is now Yellowstone National Park nearly 10,000 years ago. But given the climate of Yellowstone for much of the year—numbing cold and lots of snow—the relationship early people had to this area was probably a carefully measured one. A small group of Shoshone people, known as Sheepeaters, did live in Yellowstone, probably shortly after the introduction of the horse and gun. While other tribes were quick to use both, Sheepeaters did not. This disadvantage may have led them to take up residence in such a formidable place. For the most part, though, Yellowstone appears to have been a "part-time" place, used for hunting and gathering, or for acquiring raw materials like obsidian to make high-quality spear points and arrowheads—a place, perhaps, to travel through in the fall, like the Bannock and Northern Shoshone Indians did at the end of their fishing seasons, journeying eastward to hunt bison on the plains.

Long after the arrival of Native Americans came fur trappers. In 1807, some believe John Colter detoured into the area on his way back to St. Louis, Missouri, from the Pacific, where he had ventured with the Lewis and Clark Expedition. In the years following Colter's visit, many famous mountain men came to Yellowstone to trap a variety of fur-bearing mammals, most notably the beaver, along the streams and rivers. In fewer than forty years, the freewheeling days of the fur trappers came to an end. But during those decades, mountain men gained a vast knowledge of the country, knowledge that would play an important role in laying groundwork for later expeditions.

Yellowstone's era of exploration—a time when people came looking not for profit (at least not directly), but for information—began in May 1860 when the party of Army Captain William Raynolds, led by legendary mountain man Jim Bridger, attempted to investigate the Yellowstone Plateau. Unfortunately, the Raynolds Expedition never accomplished its goal, as the party was forced back by deep snows in the high country. Efforts to explore what is now Yellowstone slowed to a crawl during the Civil War, but in 1869 a group of private citizens from Montana Territory set off on a month-

This jumble of sticks may have been built by Sheepeaters. The Sheepeaters built similar structures, called wickiups, to use as shelter. MICHAEL SAMPLE

long journey through Yellowstone. Again, the purpose was merely to see what the region contained. The Cook-Folsom-Peterson Expedition, as it was called, was a bold adventure, made more so by the men's decision to travel without an Army escort. The notes and maps created by these citizens helped General Henry Washburn, the new Surveyor General of Montana, launch his own exploratory efforts the following summer. Legend has it that on Washburn's trip, a historic campfire conversation took place, during which the idea first arose that this fantastic place should be withdrawn from settlement and declared a national park. On December 18, 1871, a bill was introduced in Congress for the establishment of such a preserve on the headwaters of the Yellowstone River; President Grant signed the measure the following spring. The world's very first national park was born.

Yellowstone National Park's early years were not trouble free. Poachers were common, tourists were robbed on occasion, and vandals routinely defaced or stole a wide variety of natural features. Within a few years of its creation, many people were saying Yellowstone should be in the hands of the Army, which could better handle such problems. The Army finally took over in 1886, and it was an important step. In those early years no one had a clear idea what the steering philosophy of a national park should be. Which activities should be allowed, and which ones should not? The Army offered stability and protection for the park while such management guidelines were being forged.

The protection afforded by the Army, as well as some

remarkable road-building efforts by the Army Corps of Engineers, allowed tourism to flourish. Soon railroads were bringing visitors from around the country to the gateway communities of Gardiner and West Yellowstone, Montana, and Cody and Lander, Wyoming, where many would set off on park tours by stagecoach and surrey cart. Access by railroad, combined with travel opportunities afforded by the automobile (car travel in the park officially began in 1915), ensured Yellowstone would be discovered and, in time, become one of America's favorite places.

In 1918, administration of Yellowstone was handed over to the newly created National Park Service, which manages the park today. ॐ

Park officials at first resisted opening Yellowstone to automobiles, fearful the machines would frighten the horses used to pull the wagons, stagecoaches, and surrey carts that conveyed tourists around the park. Two months before the park relented and Yellowstone officially opened its gates to motorists in 1915, a Franklin and a Buick were driven around the Grand Loop, satisfying the acting superintendent that cars could indeed handle the steep grades. Behind the car in this photograph is the Old Faithful Inn, one of the most famous log buildings in the world, designed by Robert Reamer. JACK E. HAYNES, courtesy MONTANA HISTORICAL SOCIETY

Climate, Vegetation, and the Yellowstone Ecosystem

*T*he types of trees and plants you will find growing in any particular part of Yellowstone are not determined by chance. Every tree, shrub, grass, and wildflower has evolved to grow best in specific environments or vegetation zones.

Basically, two main forces determine the species in any given vegetation zone. The first is the amount of rain and snowfall that occurs in the area. Cooler air at higher elevations cannot hold as much moisture as warmer air at lower elevations. As a result, the higher in elevation you go in the park, the more precipitation there is likely to be as the clouds shed excess moisture. The process is made a bit more complicated, however, by something called a rain shadow. Moist air masses arriving from the west are pushed upward by uplands located in the southwest corner of the park; as these air masses rise they grow cooler, resulting in precipita-

tion in this area. This tends to leave less moisture available to fall on lands lying on the lee, or rain-shadow side, of those southwest highlands.

The second determining factor for plant habitat in Yellowstone is soil type—in particular, the mineral content and water-holding capacity of the soil. Lodgepole pine, for instance, does well in the volcanic soil known as rhyolite, but faces a lot of competition from spruce and fir trees in Yellowstone's other main type of soil, Absaroka volcanics. The other trees (spruce, fir, and Douglas-fir) do not grow very well in the poor rhyolite soils.

Biologists have divided the park into three major vegetation zones. The largest of the major zones is called "spruce-fir," the next largest is "lodgepole," and the third, "Douglas-fir." These names refer to the trees that would dominate the area if no fires occurred for more than 300 years. But fire is a major part of the Yellowstone environment, and lodgepole pine colonizes burns very well and grows faster than the other tree species. Therefore, about 60 percent of the park is covered by lodgepole pine trees. There are two smaller zones: "alpine tundra," existing at elevations above roughly 10,000 feet, and "Great Basin vegetation," found at low elevations in a small area near Gardiner, Montana.

Mix the topography, soil type, and climate together; add the tremendous array of life forms those conditions support; and you get the marvelously complex set of links, or relationships, we call an ecosystem.

Yellowstone National Park actually makes up less than one-sixth of the entire Yellowstone ecosystem. It is important to keep in mind that much of what happens outside park borders can greatly affect life inside. Soil erosion occurring outside the park, for example, can silt streams that flow into the park, thus damaging its fisheries. Noxious weeds are sometimes brought into surrounding national forests through contaminated horse feed; they flourish and, in time, take root in Yellowstone, choking out native plants. Yellowstone's elk herds may suffer if winter range is lost to human development outside the park. And tapping into thermal springs beyond Yellowstone's borders could have consequences for the park's geysers. ☙

YELLOWSTONE'S VEGETATION ZONES

Douglas-fir Zone

Lodgepole Pine Zone

Spruce-fir Zone

ILLUSTRATION BY PETER GROSSHAUSER.

Pelican Valley is typical of Yellowstone's high altitude valleys which provide critical habitat for fish, birds, and grazing mammals. The upper reaches of the valley also contain some of the best grizzly bear habitat anywhere in the continental United States. JEFF AND ALEXA HENRY

WHAT TO KNOW BEFORE YOU GO

Driving Times: You might at first think the driving times listed at the beginning of each road segment are more generous than they need to be since the speed limit on most park roads is 45 miles per hour. But keep in mind that this is a place where bison, moose, and a host of other wildlife have free run of the roads; where bear, elk, and coyote "jams" are common; and where excited visitors sometimes forget their traffic manners in their quest for the perfect photograph. (Please do not add to this problem. Park in designated areas off the road, and close your car doors to make passage by other cars and people easier.) All driving times listed in this guide are approximate and do not include stops.

Wildlife: The privilege of enjoying Yellowstone's array of wild creatures comes with a responsibility to respect the space those animals need to feel safe and free of unnecessary stress. Never approach or otherwise breach the comfort zone of a wild animal. Not for a picture. Not for a better look. Moose, bison, and even elk, can turn aggressive, and all are quite capable of severely injuring or killing you. Bears, although they normally avoid humans, are also a danger to visitors. Every year a sur-

prising number of visitors end up in area clinics and hospitals with serious injuries resulting from getting too close to wild animals. Even small mammals can issue nasty bites if they feel threatened. Some small animals, such as ground squirrels, do not appear to be threatened, but will still bite. For your own safety and that of your friends and family—and certainly for the welfare of the animals you have come to spend time with—keep your distance.

Thermal Features: As you explore Yellowstone's geothermal areas, you will notice trails consisting of boardwalks or asphalt. This is not just to minimize ground disturbance. Since many geothermal areas have very thin crusts, such walkways also allow safe passage. Even a child can break through this delicate crust, resulting in serious burns from steam or scalding water. Watch children very carefully. Stay on the boardwalks at all times, and please remember that pets are not allowed in thermal areas. Putting any object in a thermal feature is illegal and harmful to the feature. Also, avoid permanent damage to cameras and eyeglasses by wiping off any of the silica-rich waters that may spray on lenses during geyser eruptions. ▪▪

CAMPING AND LODGING

As you might have guessed, Yellowstone is a very popular place. Park campgrounds usually fill up by 10 A.M. in mid-summer. If you are planning to camp in one of these facilities, you will need to secure your spot early. Similarly, reservations for dinner at the major hotel dining rooms should be made as early as possible.

Seven of the twelve campgrounds in Yellowstone National Park are operated by the National Park Service and are open on a first-come, first-served basis. They are Indian Creek, Lewis Lake, Mammoth, Norris, Pebble Creek, Slough Creek, and Tower Fall. The remaining campgrounds are operated by Amfac Parks and Resorts, and are located at Bridge Bay, Canyon Village, Grant Village, Madison, and Fishing Bridge RV Park. You can reserve space in these latter facilities by calling Amfac Parks and Resorts at 307-344-7311.

The only campground offering water, sewer, and electrical hookups is located at Fishing Bridge. Because of bear activity, this facility is for hard-sided vehicles only (no tents or pop-up tent trailers). No vehicle camping is allowed outside of designated campgrounds.

Camping in areas outside of campgrounds listed here

(backcountry camping) requires a permit. Most backcountry campsites can be reserved in advance, although a portion of the sites is always available for campers without reservations. For more information, call 307-344-7381 or write: Backcountry Office, P.O. Box 168, Yellowstone National Park, WY 82190.

For reservations at any of Yellowstone's nine lodging facilities, call Amfac Parks and Resorts at 307-344-7311. Lodging is generally open throughout the park from early May through late October, although this may vary from year to year. Reservations should be made up to six months in advance for peak periods. Park lodging closes from late October until December, when park roads re-open to oversnow vehicles. From December to early March lodging is available only at Mammoth Hot Springs and at Old Faithful. Lodging is also available in the gateway communities of Gardiner and West Yellowstone, Montana, and Cody and Jackson, Wyoming. Information about these locations can be obtained from the chamber of commerce for each town. Gas, film, camping supplies, and groceries are generally available in the park where hotels and visitor centers are located. ▪▪

the Entrance Roads

*Y*ou will enter Yellowstone by one of the five entrance roads described in this book. Depending on where you plan to travel after leaving the park, you can either depart the same way you came in or exit through another gateway. Entrances are on the north, west, south, and east sides of the park, as well as at the northeast corner. Winter auto visitors should keep in mind that while both the North and Northeast entrances, and only these two, are open to wheeled vehicles, visitors must enter the park initially through the North Entrance, as the road beyond the Northeast Entrance (U.S. Highway 212) is plowed for a distance of only 4 miles, to a point just past the town of Cooke City, Montana.

The descriptions that follow take you from a park entrance to a junction with the Grand Loop road. If you decide to go in the opposite direction from the description, start at the end of the section and work backward. (In which case, of course, when you find something described "on the left," you'll need to look right.) ☙

The gorgeous sweep of the Lamar Valley with snowy Specimen Ridge in the background. MICHAEL SAMPLE

North Entrance Road
NORTH ENTRANCE TO MAMMOTH HOT SPRINGS

• Driving Time: 15 minutes • Distance: 5 miles

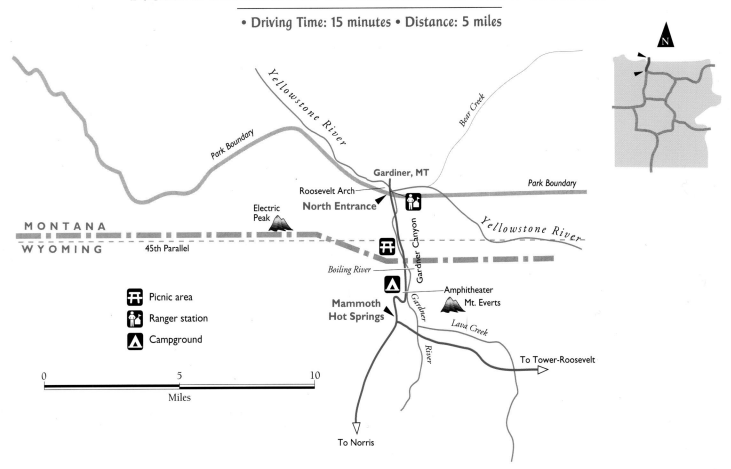

Picnic area

Ranger station

Campground

0   5   10
Miles

*T*he North Entrance Road takes you from Gardiner, Montana, into Yellowstone through the famous Roosevelt Arch. This towering, 50-foot-tall entryway constructed from blocks of basaltic stone was dedicated by President Theodore Roosevelt in April 1903 when he troweled the mortar on which the giant cornerstone was set. Over the years, this arch has become not only an important symbol of Yellowstone, but of the idea behind all of our national parks. The words inscribed on the arch—"For the Benefit and Enjoyment of the People"—make it clear that, in addition to being preserved, the park's resources are also to be made available to those who wish to visit.

Just inside the park, the road passes through the lowest, and therefore among the mildest, of Yellowstone's microclimates—and that makes this area a favorite winter habitat for pronghorn and elk. Speaking of wildlife, keep your eyes open as you make your way through the Gardner Canyon, as

bighorn sheep are known to appear along the 600-foot-high cliffs. Bighorns spend a great deal of time moving along such rugged terrain, where few predators can follow.

The Gardner River is easily visible along the early miles of this route, flowing swiftly north on its way to rendezvous with the Yellowstone River near Gardiner. Growing on its banks are clusters of cottonwoods, while on drier ground you will find both Rocky Mountain juniper and Douglas-fir. Pockets of willow crowd the floodplains. In those stretches where the river comes closest to the road, look carefully among the river rocks for a glimpse of a dark gray, wren-like bird known as a dipper. This remarkable, year-round resident of Yellowstone feeds on insects found in the beds of watercourses throughout the park. To feed, the dipper often walks underwater along the stream bottom, its wings half-outstretched to balance against the current. Kingfishers, osprey, and even bald eagles, can sometimes be seen in this same area.

The North Entrance Road enters the state of Wyoming just beyond the second crossing of the Gardner River. The state line is close to a sign along the highway that marks the 45th parallel of latitude—an imaginary line encircling the Earth, halfway between the equator and the North Pole. From here, the road continues to climb, steadily rising above the Gardner River. If you look several hundred yards to the left (east), you may see puffs of steam rising from Boiling River, the largest flowing hot spring in Yellowstone. Thought perhaps to be part of the underground outflow of Mammoth Hot Springs, Boiling River runs above ground for less than 150 yards before joining the Gardner. ⤳

The Roosevelt Arch was designed by Robert Reamer, the same architect who designed the beautiful Old Faithful Inn. The arch was erected near the railroad in the town of Gardiner, Montana; tourists would leave the train and board stagecoaches which carried them through this arch and into the national park. MICHAEL SAMPLE

Autumn brings a fresh splash of color to the skunk brush and buffalo berry along the Gardner River near Yellowstone's North Entrance. The relatively low elevation here means less snowfall, and that means easier feeding for grazing animals such as elk and pronghorn.
MICHAEL SAMPLE

West Entrance Road

WEST ENTRANCE TO MADISON

• Driving Time: 30 minutes • Distance: 14 miles

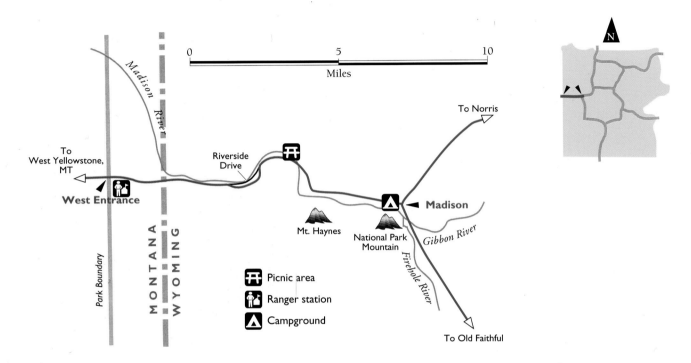

There is a wonderful gentleness to be found in this western approach to Yellowstone. The entire route is a bright meander along the cold, clear flow of the Madison River, its waters spotted with Canada geese and trumpeter swans. Along the banks are rich meadows, standing kelly green in the summer sun, their lushness a stark contrast to bald, burned-

over volcanic rocks and talus slopes rising to the south. A number of turnouts present themselves along the main route, as well as a short run of road called Riverside Drive, any of which make a perfect setting for a long, lazy lunch. Fly fishing is popular along much of the route, though anglers should be aware that parts of the river may be closed in early summer

Trumpeter swans near a nesting area on the Madison River. These magnificent birds—the largest waterfowl in North America—have very low reproduction rates; furthermore, their nesting activities are easily disrupted by humans. For this reason, park regulations prohibit anyone from coming within 25 yards (22 meters) of a swan. JEFF AND ALEXA HENRY

to protect nesting trumpeter swans; a fishing permit, available at park ranger stations, is required.

At the end of this entrance road, lying just south of the Madison Campground, is a somewhat common-looking peak called National Park Mountain. According to what most historians consider a legend, one evening during the Henry Washburn Expedition of 1870, several of the men discussed the notion that this amazing area should be removed from settlement and preserved as a park. That campfire discussion is said to have occurred at the base of this mountain. Not surprisingly, many people today consider this spot to be the birthplace of national parks. ☽

Northeast Entrance Road

NORTHEAST ENTRANCE TO TOWER-ROOSEVELT

Driving Time: 50 minutes • Distance: 29 miles

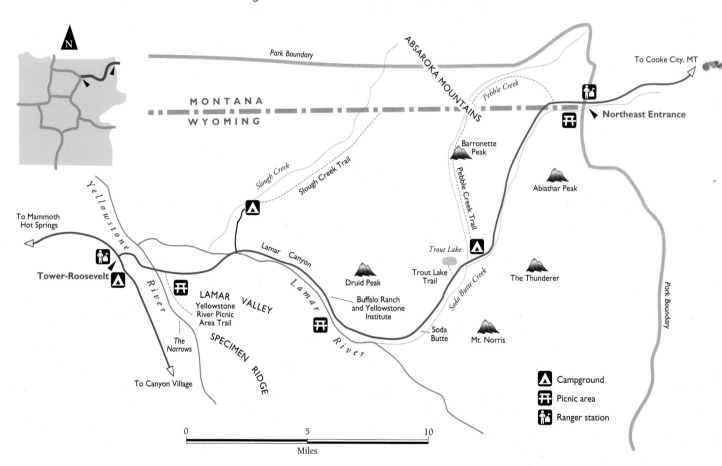

This entry road begins in a hushed forest, the quiet broken only by the murmurs of Soda Butte Creek. Before long, though, the vegetation recedes to reveal dramatic glimpses of the Absaroka Mountains—in particular, 10,404-foot Barronette Peak on the right (north) side of the road, and 10,928-foot Abiathar Peak on the left (south). From this point, the route tumbles down an ever-broadening valley. Twelve miles from the entrance you will pass Soda Butte, a remnant hot springs cone. Shortly after Soda Butte, the valley widens to embrace the Lamar River and fast becomes a sublime, yawning sweep of timothy and sage. This is wintering ground for nearly a thousand elk and hundreds of bison;

the latter can often be seen in winter, plowing into deep snow with their massive heads to get at the grass underneath. Elk and bison are also common here during spring and fall, but move to cooler, higher meadows in summer. During warmer seasons, the banks of the Lamar River are home to ducks, Canada geese, and other waterfowl.

Once past the Lamar Canyon, well to the left (south) is Specimen Ridge, containing one of the world's most famous petrified forests. Some geologists believe that, beginning some 50 million years ago, no fewer than 27 separate forests were buried under successive ancient volcanic explosions spanning a period of 20,000 years. Once the trees were covered, water seeped through the lava ash, picking up silica along the way. The silica was slowly deposited around the cells of the dead trees, petrifying them. These trees—many of them enormous and some 500 years old at the time they were buried—aren't the same species found in the park today, but speak of a time when these were much warmer, wetter lands: chestnut, persimmon, bayberry, laurel, and magnolia. Visitors who would like to see a petrified tree close up without making the grueling hike up Specimen Ridge, can find a good example at a wayside exhibit 1.5 miles west of Tower-Roosevelt. There is also a wonderful sample at Mammoth Hot Springs in front of the Albright Visitor Center. ꙮ

The Lamar Valley provides critical winter and spring range for bison and elk. In fact, the large number of elk in this valley was one of the reasons that biologists selected the Lamar as a prime release site for the reintroduction of wolves. MICHAEL SAMPLE

Soda Butte Creek, in the northeastern corner of Yellowstone National Park. The thick forests and willow banks found along the upper reaches of this stream provide ideal habitat for moose. Lower down, in more open areas like this one, look for bison, elk, and even wolves. MICHAEL SAMPLE

Rich sweeps of grass and wildflowers appear on the floors of Yellowstone forests. The pink-colored blooms here are fireweed; the yellow, daisy-like flowers are heartleaf arnica. MICHAEL SAMPLE

Northeast Entrance Road

WALKS AND HIKES

PEBBLE CREEK TRAIL

Distance: 24 miles round trip. (This hike ends along the Northeast Entrance Road; those with a shuttle car can make it a one-way trip.)

Difficulty: Moderate to difficult, depending on distance traveled.

Starting Point: Near Pebble Creek Campground, the trailhead is 8.7 miles west of the Northeast Entrance to Yellowstone, and 200 yards east of the Pebble Creek Bridge. The trail ends 8 road miles away (12 miles by trail) on the Northeast Entrance Road, at Warm Creek Trailhead/Picnic Area.

This is a strenuous hike, best suited to those in good physical condition. The Upper Meadows (reached at 9.5 miles) are especially beautiful in July and early August, when they're bedecked with colorful runs of wildflowers. (These meadows can be reached from the other end in slightly more than 2.5 miles by starting from the Warm Creek Picnic area, though that route requires you to tackle a steep climb of more than 1,000 feet in 1.5 miles.) Note that at 3 miles there are 2 crossings of Pebble Creek; before early to mid-July, the water here can be deep and swift.

SLOUGH CREEK

Distance: 22 miles round trip to the park's northern boundary and back to the trailhead.

Difficulty: Easy to moderate, depending on distance traveled.

Starting Point: 0.5 mile south of Slough Creek Campground on gravel road to campground.

After climbing through a fine slice of Douglas-fir forest, the Slough Creek Trail settles in beside the gentle, meandering Slough Creek, which is famous for its trout. A meadow is reached in fewer than 3 miles. The openness of this valley makes it a great place to watch wildlife—moose in spring; coyote, trumpeter swans, and birds of prey in summer; elk and bison during the fall.

TROUT LAKE

Distance: 1 mile round trip.

Difficulty: Moderate, due to 200-foot elevation gain in 0.25 mile.

Starting Point: Northeast Entrance Road, 1.5 miles south of Pebble Creek Campground.

This is a short, easy walk through a Douglas-fir forest to a small lake where you might spot Barrow's goldeneyes, cormorants, or eared grebes. The lake, formerly known as Fish Lake, has long been known for its good trout habitat.

YELLOWSTONE RIVER PICNIC AREA

Distance: 4 miles round trip.

Difficulty: Easy.

Starting Point: Northeast Entrance Road, 1.5 miles east of Tower-Roosevelt.

Special Note: There are steep drop-offs close to the trail. Stay on the path.

This is a perfect path for getting to know the Yellowstone River. The hike offers breathtaking views of the Narrows, a tight stretch of river canyon. You will also be able to spot the volcanic spires that rise above Tower Fall. In June, hikers should keep their eyes open for bighorn sheep.

THE WOLF RETURNS

Wolf packs disappeared from Yellowstone in the 1920s, victims of an intense extermination effort launched in a time when lay people and land managers alike considered the animals destructive predators. Then in January 1995, in one of the most exciting wildlife conservation efforts in American history, fourteen Canadian wolves were captured near Hinton, Alberta, and relocated to Yellowstone. This event, along with a simultaneous release in central Idaho, was the fruit of more than twenty-five years of intense study and preparation; truly, it marked a new level of understanding and acceptance of the roles that predators play in a healthy ecosystem.

For approximately nine weeks after their arrival in Yellowstone, the wolves were contained in three large pens in the vicinity of the Lamar Valley. Their first steps out of the pens and onto free ground came in late March 1995. Like the seventeen additional wolves brought from Canada the following year, they adapted quickly to the park, feeding on young, old, or diseased elk, just as they did in their former territories in Canada. Biologists are watching with great interest the effect of Yellowstone wolves on other park animals. Some of the Lamar Valley coyotes, for example, are being displaced into new territories by the wolves. Eagles, ravens, magpies, foxes, and grizzly bears, on the other hand, feed on elk that have been killed by wolves. This extra food may be especially helpful to grizzly bears in spring, when the bears are hungry and food is hard to find. ▪▪

Bunkhouse at the historic Buffalo Ranch, in the Lamar Valley. Classes on a wide variety of natural and cultural history subjects—wildflowers to wolves to mountain men—are offered here, through the non-profit Yellowstone Association Field Institute, sponsored by the Yellowstone Association. MICHAEL SAMPLE

THE BUFFALO RANCH

Seventeen miles west of the Northeast Entrance, on the north side of the road, is a cluster of log buildings overlooking the great sweep of the Lamar Valley. This is the Buffalo Ranch, so called because from 1907 to 1952 the area was used to rebuild bison populations through the use of captive herds. When this operation began, the North American bison was nearly extinct. The Buffalo Ranch played a critical role in the struggle to bring this magnificent animal back to at least a portion of its former range.

The barn and the bunkhouse (the long, low building to the left of the barn) can be seen from the road and are remnants of the Buffalo Ranch; however, there are no visitor services at this location. The ranch is now the base for a remarkable array of affordable natural and cultural history courses offered to the public by the non-profit Yellowstone Association Field Institute, sponsored by the Yellowstone Association. Prior registration is required; for information about how to participate, call 307-344-2294.

Expedition Yellowstone, an educational program offered by the National Park Service to school groups, is also based at the Buffalo Ranch. ▪▪

Wolves were returned to Yellowstone in 1995 after an absence of nearly seventy years and are now thriving here. Wolf populations in and around Yellowstone are expected to stabilize at roughly 100 to 125 animals. NATIONAL PARK SERVICE PHOTO

East Entrance Road

EAST ENTRANCE TO FISHING BRIDGE

• Driving Time: 1 hour • Distance: 27 miles

N

To Canyon Village

Yellowstone River

Howard Eaton Trail

Pelican Creek

Fishing Bridge

Amphitheater

Visitor Center/ Yellowstone Assoc. Bookstore

(Hard-sided vehicles)

Pelican Creek Trail

Storm Point Trail

Picnic area

Ranger station

Store

Campground

Lake Village

Indian Pond

Storm Point

Bridge Bay

Yellowstone Lake

Steamboat Springs

Lake Butte Overlook

To West Thumb

RANGE

Cody Peak

Avalanche Peak

Hoyt Peak

To Cody, WY

Clear Creek

Sylvan Lake

Sylvan Pass

East Entrance

Grizzly Peak

Eleanor Lake

Middle Creek

Top Notch Peak

West Thumb

Mt. Doane

Mt. Langford

Mt. Stevenson

ABSAROKA

Park Boundary

0   5   10

Miles

*O*f all entryways into Yellowstone, none seems more a celebration of the high country than this one. In the first 7 miles, the road twists upward through the forest along Middle Creek to a height of 8,541 feet, brushing the base of Top

Notch Peak at Sylvan Pass. Top Notch, in addition to Hoyt Peak to the north, is part of a magnificent, 80-mile-long line of mountains known as the Absaroka Range.

Once over Sylvan Pass, the road descends through forest

Steamboat Springs, at Steamboat Point, on the shore of Yellowstone Lake. Early explorers and visitors alike routinely linked Yellowstone's thermal vents and geysers to the sights and sounds they'd come to associate with steamboats. (This feature is not to be confused with Steamboat Geyser, which is located in the Back Basin of the Norris Geyser Basin.) ERWIN AND PEGGY BAUER

past the hush of Eleanor and Sylvan Lakes. About 16 miles from the East Entrance, a side road leads to Lake Butte Overlook on the right. From the Lake Butte vantage point, some 600 feet above the water, you can look across the great caldera, Yellowstone Lake, and all the way to the Teton Mountains, 60 miles to the left (southwest). Farther to your right (northwest), is a cluster of handsome peaks known as the Washburn Range, one of only two mountain ranges contained entirely within the park. From this point, the East Entrance Road descends to the shore of Yellowstone Lake, passing a thermal area known as Steamboat Springs. Finally, the road tracks across a magnificent waterfowl area fanning out from the banks of Pelican Creek.

The Fishing Bridge Museum and Visitor Center is located

on the East Entrance Road, 1 mile east of the Grand Loop. The museum's displays offer a wonderful overview of the birds of Yellowstone. You can also view specimens of river otters, as well as a grizzly bear and cubs. Books, maps, and other interpretive material are offered in the non-profit Yellowstone Association bookstore in the east wing of the building. ☙

East Entrance Road

WALKS AND HIKES

PELICAN CREEK TRAIL

Distance: 1 mile round trip.

Difficulty: Easy.

Starting Point: 1 mile east of Fishing Bridge Visitor Center, at the west end of Pelican Creek Bridge.

This delightful path guides you through woods to the shore of Yellowstone Lake before looping back across a fabulous marsh, rich with life. As you walk this latter stretch, keep an eye peeled for pelicans, Canada geese, mallards, great blue heron, ospreys, and bald eagles.

The tranquillity of Sylvan Lake, with Top Notch Peak in the background. Top Notch is part of the volcanic Absaroka Range. The upper reaches of this mountain, like several other areas around Sylvan Pass, contain fine examples of petrified forests. JEFF HENRY

STORM POINT TRAIL

Distance: 3 miles round trip.

Difficulty: Easy.

Starting Point: 2.5 miles east of the Fishing Bridge Visitor Center, departing from the turnout at Indian Pond.

This walk begins beside Indian Pond, a feature geologists refer to as a hydrothermal explosion crater. Long ago, there was a pocket of very hot water here. The water was kept from boiling over by intense pressure against it, possibly from the water of a glacial lake. One theory is that the lake drained, rapidly decreasing the pressure (like taking the lid off a pressure cooker), thus allowing the water to flash into steam with such force that it blasted out the crater that would become Indian Pond. From the pond, the trail winds through forest and out onto Storm Point, which offers breathtaking views of Yellowstone Lake.

HOWARD EATON TRAIL

Distance: Variable, as trail traverses much of the park.

Difficulty: Easy.

Starting Point: In the parking lot at the east end of Fishing Bridge.

This path winds north for 15 miles, all the way to Canyon Village, generally paralleling the river; the northernmost 12 miles are not well maintained. The quietest stretch (as far as highway noise) is the first 2 miles, which offer a nice mix of meadow, forest, and riparian areas along the Yellowstone River. (A riparian area is the zone of life that exists along the banks of a natural watercourse.) This is an especially good area for bird watching; be alert for bears.

Indian Pond, on the shore of Yellowstone Lake, was a favorite camping area for early native peoples. It was close to fine hunting grounds in Pelican Valley and fishing opportunities in Yellowstone Lake. MICHAEL SAMPLE

South Entrance Road

SOUTH ENTRANCE TO WEST THUMB

• Driving Time: 50 minutes • Distance: 22 miles

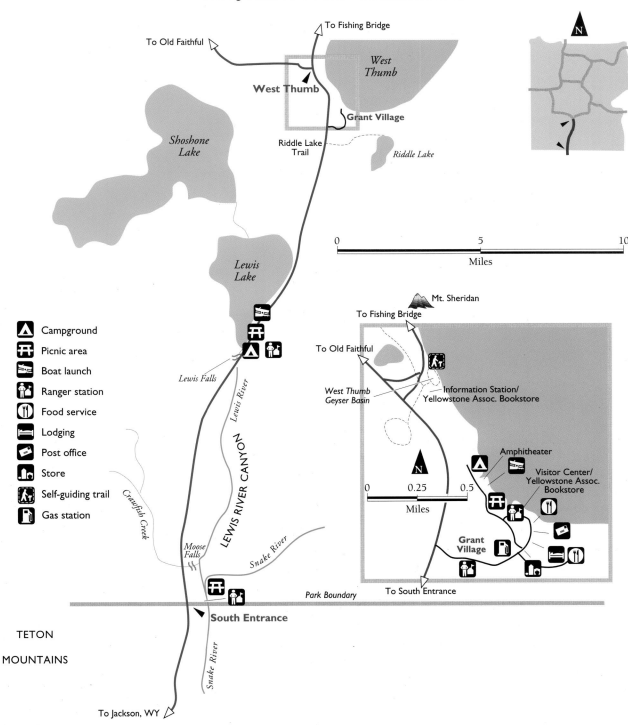

Campground
Picnic area
Boat launch
Ranger station
Food service
Lodging
Post office
Store
Self-guiding trail
Gas station

*F*ewer than 2 miles north of the southern entry point to the park on the right (east) side of the road is a small turnoff for Moose Falls, a braided tumble of water formed by Crawfish Creek as it makes a headlong plunge toward the Lewis River. (Thanks to upstream thermals, Crawfish Creek contains the largest crawfish population in the park.) From this point on along the drive, you will have several fine views of the Lewis Canyon, which was carved by the Lewis River out of the enormous welded-ash flows that roared out of the Yellowstone Caldera. Beyond the head of this canyon is yet another Lewis River work of art—37-foot-high Lewis Falls, pounding past dark, rich shadows of a coniferous forest.

Just above these falls is Lewis Lake, named for that intrepid explorer Meriwether Lewis. In 1804 Lewis, with William Clark, led one of the most remarkable expeditions in American history, exploring lands acquired in the Louisiana Purchase. In truth, the party never got closer than 50 miles from what would become Yellowstone, so Lewis never actually saw his namesake lake. From Lewis Lake, it is about 6 miles to Grant Village. Turn right into the Grant Village area and travel about a mile to the visitor center, where you will find an excellent exhibit on the role that fire plays in the Yellowstone ecosystem, as well as a Yellowstone Association bookstore. A general store, hotel, gas station, and restaurant are also located in Grant Village. Several miles beyond the turn-off to Grant Village, you will join the Grand Loop Road at West Thumb. ꙮ

Facing page: Although this cow moose has only one calf, twins are not unusual. A cow moose defending a calf can be very aggressive and will sometimes charge humans. CAROL POLICH

Autumn comes to the Lewis River. One of the many tributaries of the Snake River, this beautiful watercourse flows from Lewis Lake, named in honor of the intrepid explorer, Meriwether Lewis. Lewis River trout are regular fare for both osprey and bald eagles.
JEFF FOOTT

South Entrance Road

WALKS AND HIKES

RIDDLE LAKE

Distance: 5 miles round trip.

Difficulty: Easy to moderate (due to distance).

Starting point: Approximately 2.2 miles south of the Grant Village turnoff, on the South Entrance Road.

Special Note: This trail is closed from approximately April 30 to July 14 to protect grizzly bears. Some parts of the trail may be wet until late July. Be sure you have appropriate shoes and mosquito repellent.

This is generally a flat walk through wonderful moose habitat, ending at the north shore of Riddle Lake, where Canada geese, Barrow's goldeneyes, and white pelicans are sometimes seen. There are fine views of Mount Sheridan from the north shore.

the Grand Loop

In the summer of 1883, thirty-one-year-old Dan Kingman had packed his bags and was on his way to West Point, when Civil War General Philip Sheridan informed the young lieutenant that he had a rather different destination in mind for him: the wilds of Yellowstone. It would fall to Kingman, a talented officer in the Army Corps of Engineers, to construct and maintain roads and bridges in Yellowstone. The "figure-8," double-track wagon road that he designed and built to provide access to Yellowstone's extraordinary attractions became known as the Grand Loop. To this day, it remains the primary corridor of travel within the park. The descriptions that follow are designed to take you along this "figure-8" loop system, from one major intersection to the next. If you decide to go in the opposite direction from the description, simply start at the end of the section and work backward. (In which case, of course, when you find something described "on the left," you'll need to look right.) ☙

Above right: Elk are frequent visitors to the Mammoth area, especially during the winter months.
MICHAEL SAMPLE

Facing page: Few things in nature are more a work in progress than the marvelous jumble of travertine known as the Mammoth Terraces. Both the amount and direction of the hot water flowing here changes daily, drying up some features, and bringing new ones to life.
MICHAEL SAMPLE

Mammoth Hot Springs to Norris

• Driving Time: 40 minutes • Distance: 21 miles

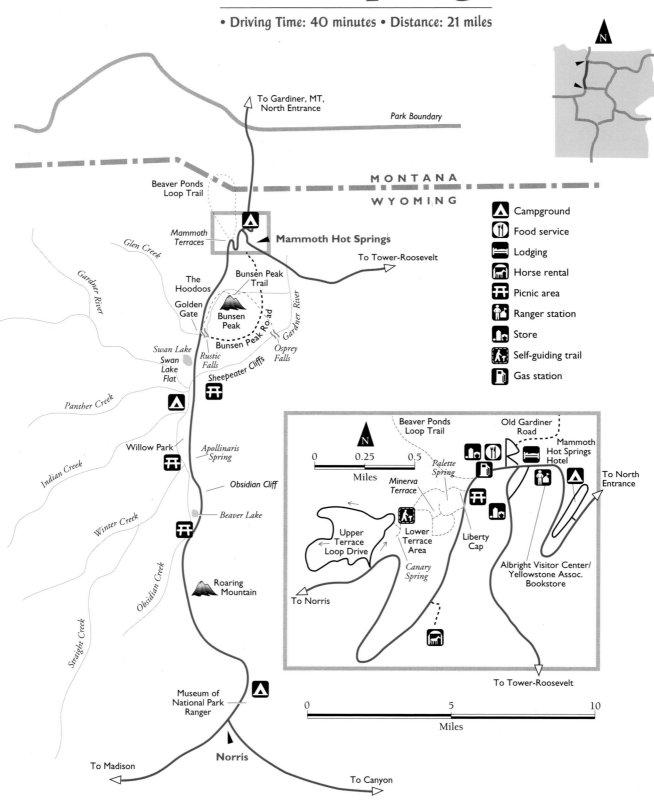

To Gardiner, MT, North Entrance

Park Boundary

Beaver Ponds Loop Trail

MONTANA
WYOMING

Campground
Food service
Lodging
Horse rental
Picnic area
Ranger station
Store
Self-guiding trail
Gas station

Mammoth Terraces
Mammoth Hot Springs

Glen Creek

To Tower-Roosevelt

The Hoodoos
Bunsen Peak Trail
Golden Gate
Bunsen Peak
Gardner River
Bunsen Peak Road
Osprey Falls

Gardner River

Swan Lake
Swan Lake Flat
Rustic Falls
Sheepeater Cliffs

Panther Creek

Willow Park
Apollinaris Spring

Indian Creek

Obsidian Cliff

Winter Creek

Beaver Lake

Obsidian Creek

Roaring Mountain

Straight Creek

Museum of National Park Ranger

Norris

To Madison

To Canyon

Inset map

Beaver Ponds Loop Trail
Old Gardiner Road
Mammoth Hot Springs Hotel

N

0   0.25   0.5
Miles

Palette Spring

Minerva Terrace

To North Entrance

Upper Terrace Loop Drive

Lower Terrace Area

Liberty Cap

Canary Spring

Albright Visitor Center/
Yellowstone Assoc.
Bookstore

To Norris

To Tower-Roosevelt

0   5   10
Miles

Facing page: In the distant past, terraces similar to these existed throughout the Mammoth Hot Springs area, on the hillside where you see them today, and near the Gardner River. CAROL POLICH

We begin in Mammoth Hot Springs at the Albright Visitor Center, where the Yellowstone Association offers a wealth of interpretive brochures and books, and park rangers offer personal advice to make your forays more enjoyable. You will also find an excellent movie and some fine exhibits spotlighting Yellowstone history, including a collection of stunning original watercolor sketches of Yellowstone by Thomas Moran—an artist who accompanied early expeditions to the park.

From the visitor center, the road to Norris climbs south past the Mammoth Terraces, a magnificent set of travertine steps. The natural chemistry and plumbing that go into the building of these terraces are quite marvelous. Rain and snowmelt seep deep into the ground and are eventually warmed by heat radiating from the large chamber of magma, or molten rock, lying just 2 to 3 miles beneath the earth. At those depths, the waters come into contact with carbon dioxide released from that same magma chamber. As the carbon dioxide dissolves in the hot water, it makes a weak carbonic acid solution, which in turn dissolves the vast limestone formations lying under the surface as it seeps downslope. Once the solution reaches open air, carbon dioxide escapes. That, in turn, causes calcium carbonate to precipitate out of the water, solidifying again as a material known as travertine. The travertine in some parts of Mammoth Terraces is building up at a rate of 2 feet per year! At Minerva Terrace, roughly in the middle of the Lower Terraces, look for massive vertical columns of travertine. These may remind you of stalactites that hang from roofs of caves; in truth, they're formed in much the same way. It is interesting to note that the location of these springs and their flow rate changes often, though the total amount of water released by all springs shows little variance.

The fanciful colors you will see in many of these thermal features are not caused by travertine, which is white, but rather by masses of primitive bacteria and algae living in the water. Thus, the shades of Yellowstone's geothermal features tend to be colorful when the feature is "active" (when water is flowing), but change to a dull white or gray when changes occur under the Earth that stop the flow. You can get a better

Three-foot-deep Swan Lake, like similar shallow ponds nearby, does indeed play host on occasion to trumpeter swans.

Beyond Swan Lake Flat, the road passes Sheepeater Cliffs (once home to Yellowstone's only resident Native Americans); winds through Willow Park, an excellent place to spot moose; passes Apollinaris Spring where some of the park's first visitors used to stop for a drink of mineral water (not recommended now); and in another mile reaches Obsidian Cliff on the left (east) side of the road. While moss and lichen cover much of the rocks of Obsidian Cliff, dulling them, it is still easy to catch glimpses of the black, shiny glass, formed by rapidly cooling lava, that was so prized by early Native Americans for making points and tools.

Make your next stop at the stark, somewhat lifeless-looking flank of Roaring Mountain, also on your left (east). Roaring Mountain takes its name from a steam vent near the summit of the peak (just one of many steam vents, or fumaroles, scattered across the mountain) that used to emit a rather startling howl, easily heard by travelers on the nearby wagon road. Roaring Mountain seemed to run out of things to say around the mid-1920s. Like so many thermal features in Yellowstone, though, it may strike up another round of noise-making sometime in the future.

Four miles past Roaring Mountain, plan a visit to the Museum of the National Park Ranger, located on the road to Norris Campground. It contains a fascinating collection of exhibits that chronicle the history of the National Park Ranger from the days of the army soldier to modern times. This classic building was erected in 1908 as one of sixteen soldier outposts, all of which were to be built at a cost of not more than 100 dollars. The station remained occupied by either soldiers or rangers (the National Park Service took over in 1918) until 1959. It was made a museum in 1991. ᴔ

view of the terraces at their base, from parking areas located on your right several hundred yards past the Mammoth Hot Springs Hotel and General Store, as well as from the Upper Terrace Loop Drive, above the terraces on the right, two miles from the Albright Visitor Center. (Towing units, buses, and motor homes longer than 25 feet or 7.6 meters, are prohibited on the Upper Terrace Loop Drive.)

Just under 2 miles beyond the turnoff for the Upper Terrace Loop Drive is a stark jumble of travertine rocks called The Hoodoos—actually pieces of old hot spring terraces that tumbled down the mountain in massive landslides. From here, you will continue to climb for another mile, passing the bright orange and yellow rocks of Golden Gate, as well as a particularly nice plunge of Glen Creek known as Rustic Falls, and finally topping out at sage-covered Swan Lake Flat.

Mammoth Hot Springs to Norris

Walks and Hikes

UPPER AND LOWER MAMMOTH TERRACES SELF-GUIDING TRAIL

Distance: Short loops and spur trails link together to offer walks of varying distances, from 100 yards to roughly 1 mile.

Difficulty: Easy to difficult, depending on route chosen.

Starting point: A series of boardwalk and asphalt trails lead through the Mammoth Terraces. Trails can be accessed from the base of the terraces at three parking areas located on your right, as well as from the Upper Terrace Loop Drive, 2 miles from the Albright Visitor Center. Plain and simple, there is no better way to see the fantastic travertine terraces of Mammoth—the handiwork of some fifty hot springs—than to ramble the network of boardwalk trails linking the Upper and Lower Terraces.

Special Note: This is an area of scalding water and unstable ground. Stay on the boardwalks and asphalt trails. While walking through any thermal area, it is important to watch children closely. Although the ground beyond may look solid, in many places it is thin and extremely fragile, and can conceal pools of scalding water.

The word *terrace*, by the way, is exactly correct. At places like Minerva Terrace you will find a stunning collection of travertine-rimmed pools, of all shapes and sizes, lying in stair-step fashion.

The bizarre jumble of limestone blocks known as The Hoodoos. The name hoodoo refers to an object that can cause bad luck. Early explorers sometimes associated the Yellowstone landscape with legends and folklore about mysterious, unknown worlds.

MICHAEL SAMPLE

BEAVER PONDS

Distance: 5 miles round trip.

Difficulty: Moderate.

Starting Point: Travel past the Mammoth Hot Springs Hotel, the General Store, and the gas station. The trail will be on your right, just before Liberty Cap, a 37-foot-high travertine cone.

This low-elevation loop walk is especially inviting in May and June, when clusters of wildflowers blossom, and again in late fall, when elk have migrated from the highlands. The trail climbs for 0.5 mile up Clematis Creek to the junction with Sepulcher Mountain Trail. From here it turns right, winds through a lovely mix of aspen, Douglas-fir, and open meadows, and finally reaches a series of beaver ponds at 2.5 miles. The return path carries you 2 miles through sweeps of sagebrush to the Old Gardiner Road and back to Mammoth Hot Springs, ending behind the Mammoth Hotel.

BUNSEN PEAK

Distance: 4 miles round trip.

Difficulty: Difficult (short but steep, gaining 1,300 feet).

Starting Point: 5 miles south of Mammoth Hot Springs on the left (east) side of the highway near the start of the old Bunsen Peak Road. Walk up the road a short distance, and watch for trail markers on your left.

This is a splendid walk for those who love good views. Savor the beauty of the high peaks to the north in the Absaroka and Gallatin ranges, as well as the Yellowstone River Valley. Bicycles are allowed on Bunsen Peak Road, which departs from the same location and goes around the base of the peak.

Some geologists believe that Bunsen Peak is actually the neck of an ancient volcano. The name Bunsen honors a German physicist who spent years struggling to better understand the inner workings of geysers.
JEFF AND ALEXA HENRY

Beaver Pond and, in the distance, snow-clad peaks in the Gallatin National Forest. Appropriately, beaver still visit these ponds on occasion, as do moose, pronghorn, mule deer, and even black bear. Look for the beaver's feeding signs, which in this particular area mean gnawed bark and branches on Douglas-fir and lodgepole pines.   MICHAEL SAMPLE

In the early days, life at Fort Yellowstone could hardly be called easy. Dust, cold weather, fire fighting, policing vandals, and chasing poachers made for hard work. Nonetheless, many soldiers considered this duty a welcome relief from the long, blistering marches they'd suffered on the Great Plains and in the deserts of the American Southwest. Protection of the park was the Army's job from 1886 until 1918, when the National Park Service took over. The last troops left Yellowstone in fall 1918.

MONTANA HISTORICAL SOCIETY

FORT YELLOWSTONE

From the overlook on Upper Terrace Loop Drive, you will have a wonderful aerial view of the fine old buildings clustered around the Albright Visitor Center—part of the old Fort Yellowstone complex. After Yellowstone National Park was established in 1872, it fell victim to vandals and poachers. In 1886, the job of protecting the park was assigned to the U.S. Army. While that arrangement was supposed to be short-lived, nearly thirty years later the Army was still patrolling roads and chasing poachers, a decision having been made to keep them on the job and to replace their temporary quarters with permanent ones. Especially beautiful are the stone buildings, seven of which were constructed in 1909 by Scottish masons using sandstone from a quarry located between Mammoth Hot Springs Campground and the Gardner River. Included in these seven buildings is the Albright Visitor Center, which originally served as quarters for bachelor officers. In 1918, the National Park Service took over management of the park. Today, the stone buildings house the main park offices; park employees live in many of the frame buildings. ▪▪

These large, many-chimneyed buildings just south of the Albright Visitor Center in Mammoth Hot Springs are handsome reminders of historic Fort Yellowstone. On their arrival in the park, most army officers believed their stay here would be a short one. But four long, cold winters spent in a temporary post were enough to prompt the construction of these more permanent facilities.

MICHAEL SAMPLE

Norris to Madison

• Driving Time: 30 minutes • Distance: 14 miles

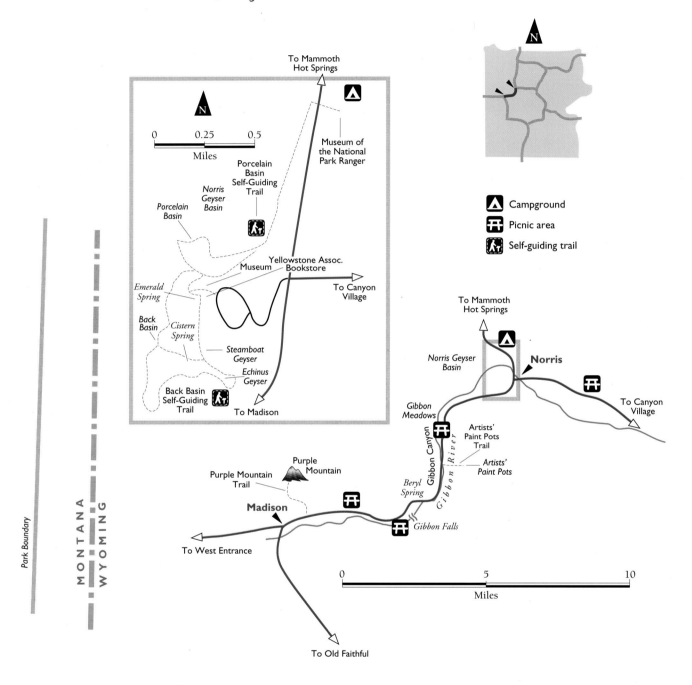

For that feeling that only Yellowstone can offer—the sense that the world is still reeling in a primordial soup of creation, caught up in some kind of marvelous conflict between inner and outer Earth—absolutely nothing beats a visit to Norris Geyser Basin. At the Norris intersection, turn right (west) on a short spur road to a large parking lot—departure point for reaching the self-guiding trails through the area's two geyser basins. To the south is Back Basin, to the north Porcelain Basin, the latter named for the beautiful white geyserite that covers a portion of the area. In the Back Basin is Steamboat Geyser, its 300- to 400-foot-high eruptions making it the tallest geyser in the world. Unfortunately,

Steamboat is very unpredictable, erupting as frequently as every four days, or sleeping months, or even years, with no activity at all.

The Norris Geyser Basin Museum is located between the geyser basins and offers a fine collection of exhibits about the features you will be seeing at Norris Geyser Basin, the perfect primer for those looking to better understand geothermal geology. Books, maps, and other interpretive materials are available for sale at the nearby Yellowstone Association bookstore.

Before you head out to the geothermal features, reread the safety information on page 14. There is scalding water here—lots of it—active not only in the features themselves, but often just underneath ground that may look solid, but is in fact nothing but a thin crust of earth that cannot support your weight. Please, for your own safety, do not step off the designated trails, and keep your children under control at all times. Finally, remember that pets are not allowed on any Yellowstone boardwalk or trail.

Evidence suggests the Norris Geyser Basin has been active for more than 100,000 years, making it the oldest thermal area in all of Yellowstone. Some of the waters found here are highly acidic, and very few register temperatures under the boiling point. In 1929, scientists drilled a test hole in this basin. At a depth of 1,087 feet (326 meters), the temperature measured an incredible 459° F.
JEFF FOOTT

The haunting beauty of Gibbon Falls. This 84-foot cascade pours down the 650,000-year-old rim of the Yellowstone Caldera.

ERWIN AND PEGGY BAUER

About 3 miles south of Norris, just past the parking area for the Artists' Paint Pots Trail, the road enters the dark reaches of Gibbon Canyon, cut by the Gibbon River through a massive lava flow of rhyolite and welded ash. At a point about 4 miles south of Norris, on the right (west) side of the road, is lovely Beryl Spring. With a temperature that hovers above the boiling point, this is one of the hottest springs in all of Yellowstone. The spring gets its name (pronounced "Burl") from a blue-green gemstone.

The Gibbon River continues to be your companion for much of this segment of the Grand Loop; at a point roughly 7 miles south of Norris, on the left (east) side of the road, the river makes a headlong 84-foot tumble, forming spectacular Gibbon Falls. This water actually falls over the rim of the Yellowstone Caldera; the rock wall on the other side of the road is a portion of the caldera's inner rim. ☙

These hot springs steam along the Artists' Paint Pots Trail where an intriguing mix of textures and colored clays awaits visitors. The term "paint pots" was used by explorers and early tourists alike to describe mud pots throughout the park. A few soldiers played on this notion, informing visitors that these were indeed the source of paint used for coating the buildings at Fort Yellowstone.

MICHAEL SAMPLE

THE FOUR TYPES OF THERMAL FEATURES

Geyser: A geyser is a hot spring with the intriguing habit of tossing underground water into the air. Water falling as rain or snow seeps through porous layers of rock. Eventually that water comes into contact with extremely hot rocks that have been heated by a large body of molten material, called magma, underneath the park. This hot water then rises through a series of cracks and fissures underneath the surface of the Earth. In a sense, these fissures are the "plumbing system" of a thermal feature. A geyser is the equivalent of a giant pressure cooker; even though the temperature of water deep down may be well above boiling, the weight and pressure of the water above prevents that boiling from happening. Eventually, though, the pressure builds enough to push the water in the upper reaches up and out, causing an overflow. That overflow, in turn, relieves the pressure on the super-heated water below, causing it to flash into steam. That flash, that explosion through a narrow, constricted place in the rocks, is what sends water shooting into the air.

Hot Spring: Hot springs let off enough heat by boiling or surface evaporation to avoid the kind of steam explosions common to geysers. Some of Yellowstone's hot springs take the form of quiet pools. Others are flowing. The waters of many of this latter type, such as those at Mammoth Hot Springs, become charged with carbon dioxide while underground, creating a mild carbonic acid. That acid dissolves underground limestone rocks and carries the mixture to the surface of the Earth. Once on the surface, the carbon dioxide gas escapes. Without carbon dioxide, the water is less able to carry the dissolved limestone. The dissolved limestone precipitates out, creating beautiful travertine terraces. In areas underlaid with volcanic rock, as opposed to more easily dissolved limestone, a modification of the plumbing system—perhaps through small earthquakes—can easily turn a hot spring into a geyser.

Fumarole (also called steam vent): In simplest terms, a fumarole is a vent in the Earth's crust. The supply of water around fumaroles is not as plentiful as in hot springs and geysers. Modest amounts of groundwater come into contact with hot rocks underground and are turned to steam. This steam rushes up through a series of cracks and fissures and out the vent, sometimes with enough force to create a loud hiss or roar.

Mudpot: In this feature, steam rises through groundwater that has dissolved surrounding rocks into clay; various minerals in the rocks make wide variations in the color of the mud. More often than not, such water is quite acidic, which helps the breaking down and dissolving process. ▪▪

ILLUSTRATION BY PETER GROSSHAUSER.

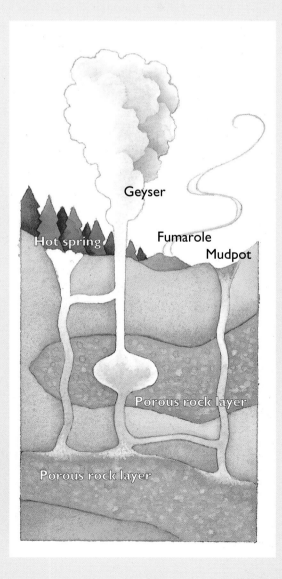

Norris to Madison

WALKS AND HIKES

BACK BASIN SELF-GUIDING TRAIL

Distance: 1.5 miles round trip.

Difficulty: Easy.

Starting Point: Follow the signs located on the south side of the Norris Geyser Basin Museum, just past the Yellowstone Association bookstore.

The Back Basin Self-Guiding Trail will introduce you to such treasures as Echinus Geyser, which, at least for the time being, is erupting on a regular schedule of thirty-five to seventy-five minutes. Echinus is the largest known acid-water geyser on Earth. (The pH of the water tests out just above vinegar!) In addition, Echinus offers one of the best opportunities in Yellowstone to study how geysers work, close up. Just prior to eruption, superheated water expands and is pushed out to pool around the mouth of the geyser. This relieves pressure from water underneath, allowing it to boil, and then finally erupt. Notice how, after the eruption, the water drains back down into the ground, and the whole cycle begins again.

In addition to Echinus, there is plenty along this walk for those fond of the striking colors often found in thermal basins (the result of both minerals and micro-organisms). For starters, visit Cistern Spring, located along the middle section of the figure-8-shaped walkway, and then Emerald Spring, just south of the museum. It is interesting to note that the northwest corner of this walkway system follows almost exactly the old Grand Loop Road. In fact, a stagecoach loading dock was located near Minute Geyser, a feature that once sported impressive eruptions. Over the years, people waiting for the stage threw so much debris in Minute Geyser that it forever altered its activity.

PORCELAIN BASIN SELF-GUIDING TRAIL

Distance: 0.75 mile round trip.

Difficulty: Easy, dirt and boardwalk.

Starting Point: Walk from the parking area at Norris to the Norris Geyser Basin Museum, and go through the breezeway (heading north). Follow the signs.

The hundreds of features in Porcelain Basin are much more concentrated than in Back Basin. As of this writing, Whirligig and Constant Geysers are favorites, primarily for the sheer frequency of their eruptions. However, they too could change dramatically in a matter of days—reminders that this basin, like so much of Yellowstone, is a work in progress. Notice how many of the pools in Porcelain Basin have a cloudy, milky look—the result of suspended particles of silica and clay. You will also find some of the edges of the pools are rimmed with patches of orange, a color that occurs when iron mixes with other elements, such as arsenic. The entire Porcelain Basin offers an eclectic mix of strange sounds, colors, and smells.

Echinus Geyser, located in the Back Basin of the Norris Geyser Basin, is the tallest predictable geyser in the Norris area. Its name (pronounced "ee KI nus") comes from a Latin term for a spiny sea urchin. The scientist who chose that name in 1878 said the pebbles in the basin reminded him of that sea creature. MICHAEL SAMPLE

Fumaroles (steam vents) whiten the sky around Porcelain Basin. Periodically (usually in the fall), the Norris Geyser Basin undergoes a large-scale change, known as a disturbance. Though no one knows for sure why these disturbances occur, they bring remarkable temporary changes to many of the features, altering color, acidity, temperature, and eruption patterns. JEFF FOOTT

ARTISTS' PAINT POTS

Distance: 1 mile round trip.

Difficulty: Easy, with one steep, sometimes rutted, uphill climb at the end.

Starting Point: 2.8 miles south of Norris, at the southern end of Gibbon Meadows, on the left (east) side of the road.

This delightful walk leads you first via boardwalk across a wet meadow, through a partially burned lodgepole forest. At the end awaits a modest but surprisingly colorful thermal area, dotted with mudpots, steam vents, and small geysers. Two mudpots at the top of the hill provide one of the best close-up views of mudpots in Yellowstone. Many of the bright colors you see are the result of a concentration of iron oxide.

PURPLE MOUNTAIN TRAIL

Distance: 6 miles round trip.

Difficulty: Difficult.

Starting Point: About 11.7 miles south of Norris, on the right side of the road.

For those feeling energetic, this trail offers nice views of the lower Gibbon, upper Madison, and Firehole Valleys, as well as of the Teton Mountains on a clear day. The path climbs 1,500 feet through scattered burned lodgepole forest, ending on the summit of Purple Mountain (8,433 feet).

Madison to Old Faithful

• Driving Time: 35 minutes • Distance: 16 miles

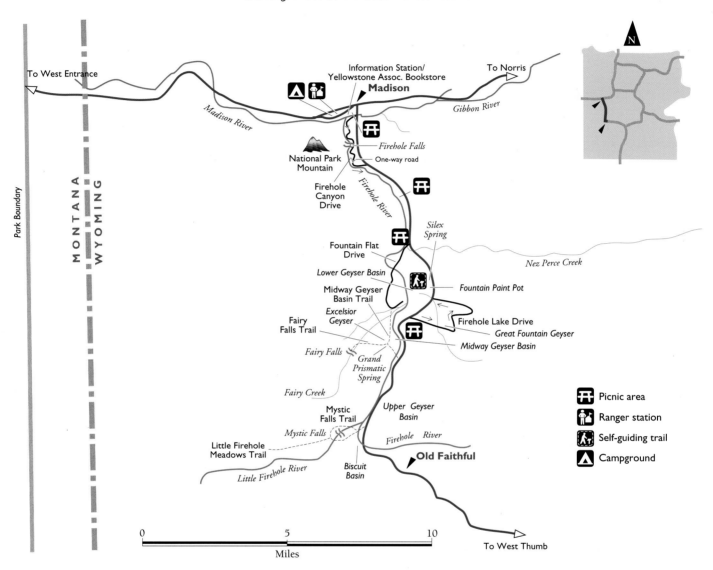

At Madison you will find a shaded picnic area and the Madison Information Station. This stone and log structure, built in 1929 and 1930, was one of the park's original road-side museums, but now serves as an information station and Yellowstone Association educational bookstore. Just south of Madison on the right (west) side of the road, is the turnoff for a beautiful, one-way drive along the Firehole River. Shortly after leaving the main road the route follows the Firehole, directly across from a spectacular vertical wall of volcanic rhyolite that rises from the west bank. From here the road

climbs above the river, offering fine views of numerous cascades and waterfalls, including 40-foot-high Firehole Falls.

Shortly after the drive rejoins the Grand Loop, the road passes Nez Perce Creek, a name that recalls the 800 men, women, and children who in 1877 fled from pursuing Army troops up this drainage, part of an astonishing 1,300-mile-long flight that began in the Wallowa Valley in Oregon.

Just south of Nez Perce Creek is Lower Geyser Basin, the first of three extraordinary basins that contain the lion's share of the world's geysers. The Lower Basin, located 8 miles south

Bison along the Firehole River. This watercourse is one of the best-loved fishing streams in all of Yellowstone. MICHAEL SAMPLE

of Madison, is where you will find Fountain Paint Pot. This colorful area offers short walks to pools and geysers, as well as to Fountain Paint Pot itself, which is Yellowstone's most famous mudpot. A one-way road, known as Firehole Lake Drive, begins 1.2 miles farther south. This 2-mile-long route will carry you past magnificent Great Fountain Geyser. Though on average Great Fountain erupts to a height of 100 feet, it occasionally lets loose with "superbursts" 200 feet high.

As hardy as geological features might seem, many have fallen victim to the bad habits of some visitors, who have broken off pieces of terraces and geyser cones for souvenirs, or tossed items into thermal features. This debris is sometimes sufficient to completely plug up the plumbing; some features never recover from the abuse. Throwing any object into a thermal feature is illegal and harmful to the feature.

Protecting Yellowstone's natural treasures sometimes has unexpected benefits. In the 1960s Dr. Thomas Brock, a professor from the University of Wisconsin, found a number of bacteria thriving in a hot spring near Great Fountain Geyser. One of those organisms, *Thermus aquaticus*, is today used widely in medical diagnosis (HIV, for instance) and as the driver of the chain reaction scientists use to carry out DNA screening and fingerprinting. It has become the basis of a 300 million-dollar industry. Some scientists believe that the hot water features of Yellowstone may contain thousands of other micro-organisms that may one day prove useful to humans.

Nine-and-a-half miles south of Madison is the parking

Great Fountain Geyser in the Lower Geyser Basin is a favorite among many Yellowstone visitors. Although the interval between eruptions is long—currently between 10 and 14 hours—it remains fairly predictable.

MICHAEL SAMPLE

The Firehole River makes a slow meander through the Midway Geyser Basin. Mountain man Jim Bridger, a great lover of tall tales, liked to say this stream was warm in places because it flowed so fast over the rocks that friction heated it. JEFF FOOTT

area for Midway Geyser Basin. Stop here for a good look at Grand Prismatic Spring—Yellowstone's largest hot spring in diameter, measuring 370 feet across and 120 feet deep. Also noteworthy is Excelsior Geyser, ringed by a mammoth crater 200 feet across. Though there has been little action in recent years, visitors in the 1880s reported eruptions at Excelsior of 300 feet.

Finally, in the third and final basin, the Upper Geyser Basin, you will find not only Old Faithful, but fully 20 percent of the world's known geysers! The description of this area can be found in the next section, Old Faithful to West Thumb. ✎✎

Welcome to the eerie world of Fountain Paint Pot. Located in the Lower Geyser Basin, this is arguably Yellowstone's most famous mudpot. Descriptions of these mud springs in the late 1800s describe them as being much more colorful than we see them today, splashed with greens and yellows and pinks—another reminder that Yellowstone is a forever-changing story. JEFF FOOTT

Madison to Old Faithful

WALKS AND HIKES

FOUNTAIN PAINT POT SELF-GUIDING TRAIL

Distance: 0.5 mile loop.

Difficulty: Easy.

Starting Point: Lower Geyser Basin, 8 miles south of Madison on the west (right) side of the road.

This easy boardwalk trail will give you a close-up look at all four kinds of Yellowstone's geothermal features: mudpots, fumaroles, geysers, and hot springs. What is more, the small hill traversed by this trail will give you a wonderful glimpse into how different thermal features form, according to how close they are to available groundwater. At the foot of the small hill, water is abundant; at Silex Spring, for example, water rises from the ground, pools, then overflows. (*Silex*, by the way, is the Latin word for silica.) But as you climb higher, you will rise above the water table, where there exists only

enough moisture to form mudpots. Here you will come across the glop and gurgle of the Fountain Paint Pot. Go farther along the trail, climb a little higher still, and suddenly there are only steam vents, or fumaroles.

MIDWAY GEYSER BASIN

Distance: 0.5 mile loop.

Difficulty: Easy.

Starting Point: Midway Geyser Basin, 9.5 miles south of Madison, on the right (west) side of the road.

This short trail by boardwalk leads to both Excelsior Geyser and Grand Prismatic Spring.

Beautiful any time of year, Yellowstone's Fairy Falls— at 197 feet, the fourth-highest named waterfall in the park—is especially striking in the thick of winter.

JEFF FOOTT

Facing page: Can you see the form of a flower in Morning Glory Pool? The most famous hot spring in Yellowstone, sadly, Morning Glory has also been one of the most heavily vandalized. Refuse tossed into the water has partially plugged the vent, allowing for a slight cooling. The cooler temperatures have in turn allowed the yellow algae to grow, which has altered the color. JEFF FOOTT

FAIRY FALLS

Distance: Approximately 5 miles round trip.

Difficulty: Easy.

Starting Point: 11.2 miles south of Madison (1 mile south of the Midway Geyser Basin), on the right (west) side of the road.

At 197 feet, this is the fourth highest named waterfall in Yellowstone. The hike follows a dirt road for about a mile, then breaks west, heading through forest for another 1.5 miles to the base of the falls. Fairy Falls truly is a delicate-looking beauty—its thin braid of white water seems to float over the rocks into the catch basin below.

MYSTIC FALLS

Distance: 2.2 miles round trip.

Difficulty: Easy to moderate.

Starting Point: 2.5 miles north of Old Faithful, in Biscuit Basin, at the west end of the basin boardwalk.

Mystic Falls is a 70-foot-high drop of the Little Firehole River. You can enjoy the falls from its base or capture a great view by climbing a series of switchbacks to the top. To turn this into a loop walk (only 0.2 mile farther), continue on the trail to the top until you reach the intersection with the Little Firehole Meadows Trail and turn right. Go past a splendid observation point, taking a moment to enjoy the distant view of Old Faithful, then continue until you rejoin the Mystic Falls Trail back to the parking area.

On the trail to Mystic Falls. Notice the lush weave of plants and young lodgepole pines sprouting in this stretch of burned forest.
MICHAEL SAMPLE

Old Faithful to West Thumb

• Driving Time: 30 minutes • Distance: 17 miles

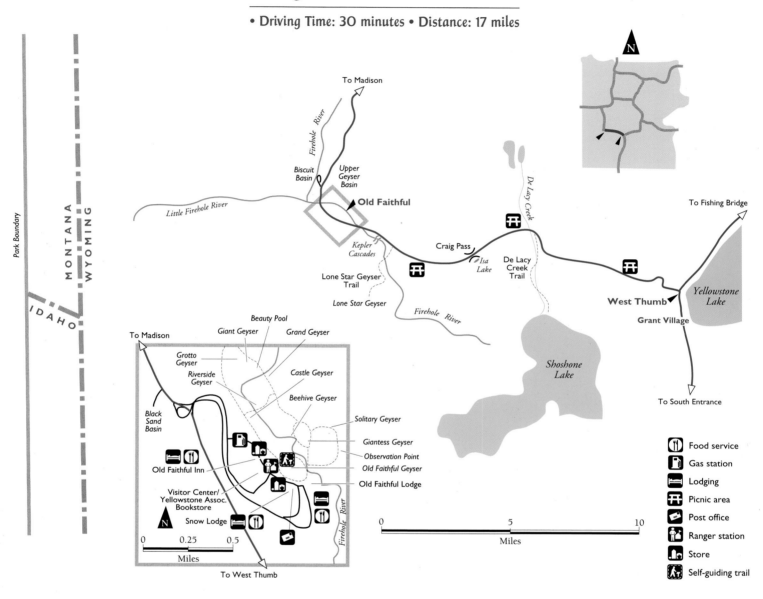

Facing page: The Old Faithful area. To the right of the famous geyser is the Old Faithful Inn and to the left the Old Faithful Lodge. The charred forest behind the complex was burned in the 1988 fires. JEFF FOOTT

*W*ithin 1 square mile of the Upper Geyser Basin are some 150 geysers, a higher concentration than anywhere else in the world. Many of these, like Old Faithful, are not only spectacular, but fairly predictable. No one knows who first laid eyes on Old Faithful Geyser, though it was given its name by members of the Washburn party, explorers who visited the region in 1870. Contrary to popular belief, Old Faithful is not the tallest geyser in the park, nor even the most predictable; honors for regularity go to Riverside Geyser, also located here in the Upper Geyser Basin on the bank of the Firehole River. (The tallest geyser in the park, and in the world, is Steamboat Geyser, located at Norris.) Nevertheless, Old Faithful is an impressive feature and certainly far more regular than most geysers. In addition, Old Faithful erupts more frequently than any of the other big geysers—twenty to twenty-three eruptions a day, with a show that lasts two to five minutes. During each eruption it discharges roughly 4,000 to 8,000 gallons of water, shooting an average of 130 feet into the air.

In the visitor center, located 200 yards from Old Faithful Geyser between the Old Faithful Inn and the Old Faithful Lodge, you will find books, maps, and other interpretive materials for sale at the Yellowstone Association bookstore, as well as an auditorium where you can see a movie about the workings of geysers. In addition, a seismograph, an instrument that records seismic activity not only in Yellowstone, but as far away as Japan, is on display. You will also want to visit the magnificent Old Faithful Inn, one of the world's best-known log structures, which is just west of the visitor center. Construction of this massive building began in 1903, and more than 500 tons of stone were used in its lobby fireplace!

Back on the Grand Loop Road beyond Old Faithful, you will come to Kepler Cascades in about 2.4 miles. From the parking area on the right, it is just a short walk to a wooden platform, where you can view Kepler's sparkling waters.

Beyond Kepler Cascades, the road bears east and goes over Craig Pass which crosses the Continental Divide at 8,261 feet. At the divide, the road passes over Isa Lake, whose waters flow to both the Atlantic and the Pacific Oceans.

This road between Old Faithful and West Thumb will carry you through an unforgettable slice of vibrant lodgepole forest. Pioneer species like aspen and lodgepole are usually first to take root after a fire, blow-down, or disease. However, shade-tolerant trees like the Engelmann spruce and Douglas-fir, the so-called climax forest, ultimately take the place of lodgepole stands and remain until a natural force, such as fire, restarts the cycle. ☽

Of the more than 300 geysers and some 10,000 other thermal features in Yellowstone National Park, none is more famous than Old Faithful Geyser. Over the years the interval between its eruptions has lengthened by a few minutes, but the blasts can still be predicted to within ten minutes.
MICHAEL SAMPLE

Beehive Geyser, located on Geyser Hill in the Upper Geyser Basin, erupts in a tight, high spray, like water from a fire hose. On being told "the beehive is playing," early visitors lounging in the Old Faithful Inn would run out of the lobby screaming with excitement. JEFF FOOTT

Old Faithful to West Thumb

WALKS AND HIKES

Special Note: Self-guiding trail leaflets are available along walkways leading to Old Faithful from the Old Faithful Inn and the visitor center. These self-guiding trail leaflets will take you along miles of boardwalks and asphalt trails through the Upper Geyser Basin. If you spend a long afternoon here, you will probably see several dramatic geyser eruptions. Before beginning your walk, check at the visitor center for anticipated eruption times of the more regular features.

OBSERVATION POINT SELF-GUIDING TRAIL

Distance: 1.1 mile loop.

Difficulty: Moderate.

Starting Point: From the Old Faithful Visitor Center, walk 0.3 mile toward Old Faithful Geyser, and then follow the board-walk that encircles the geyser counterclockwise. The trail takes off from the back (east) side of the boardwalk and crosses the Firehole River.

Those looking for the perfect place to watch Old Faithful should try the view from Observation Point, reached via a 1.1 mile loop trail. After crossing the Firehole River, you'll reach a spur trail on the right leading to Observation Point. This is a wonderful place to survey the astonishing colors, spewing water, and wisps of steam that lace the geyser basin. Your first reaction from this vantage point might be that this is a barren place, devoid of life. But as you pass the thermal features that mark the rest of this walk, take another look. White and yellow strands visible in the outflow of boiling springs are in fact bacteria. As the water cools, forms of algae appear—first yellow, then they change to dark green farther downstream. This algae, in turn, gives rise to a rich mix of insects, which in turn gives rise to spiders, dragonflies, and even birds, who feed on the lower level of insects.

Continue past Observation Point to Solitary Geyser, which once supplied water for a swimming pool at Old Faithful. From here you can join the Geyser Hill Loop Trail or turn left and follow the path back to the boardwalk around Old Faithful Geyser.

LONE STAR GEYSER

Distance: 4.8 miles round trip.

Difficulty: Easy to moderate.

Starting Point: About 2.5 miles east of the turnoff to Old Faithful from the Grand Loop Road; just beyond the Kepler Cascades parking lot.

Lone Star Geyser's 12-foot-tall cone is not only one of the largest in the park, but also one of the most beautiful, decorated with glistening pink- and silver-colored beads of sinter. Sinter, sometimes referred to as geyserite, is a substance rich in silica. For now, Lone Star erupts more faithfully than Old Faithful, sending out 40-foot-high eruptions about every 3 hours. This route is also a partially-paved bike trail as far as Lone Star Geyser; however, bicycles are not allowed off trail or beyond the geyser.

SHOSHONE LAKE VIA DE LACY CREEK

Distance: 6 miles round trip.

Difficulty: Moderate, due to distance.

Starting Point: Approximately 8.5 miles east of Old Faithful, on the Grand Loop Road.

This fairly gentle path offers the shortest route to Shoshone Lake. Along the way you will find a wonderful mix of creek, forest, and open meadows, holding everything from moose to mallards to sandhill cranes. A circuit of other trails rims the entire lake, the largest in the Yellowstone backcountry with the exception of Yellowstone Lake.

West Thumb to Fishing Bridge

• Driving Time: 45 minutes • Distance: 21 miles

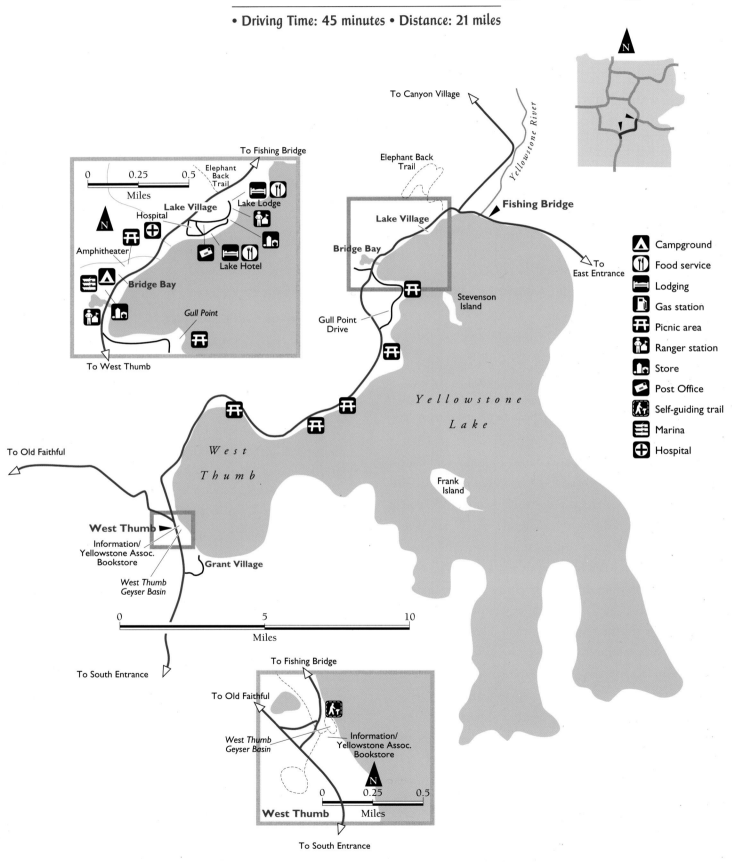

To Canyon Village

Yellowstone River

Elephant Back Trail

Fishing Bridge

To Fishing Bridge

Elephant Back Trail

Lake Village

Lake Lodge

Hospital

Amphitheater

Bridge Bay

Lake Hotel

Gull Point

Lake Village

Bridge Bay

To East Entrance

Stevenson Island

Gull Point Drive

To West Thumb

Yellowstone Lake

To Old Faithful

West Thumb

Frank Island

West Thumb

Information/
Yellowstone Assoc.
Bookstore

Grant Village

West Thumb Geyser Basin

| 0 | 5 | 10 |

Miles

To South Entrance

To Fishing Bridge

To Old Faithful

Information/
Yellowstone Assoc.
Bookstore

West Thumb Geyser Basin

| 0 | 0.25 | 0.5 |

West Thumb   Miles

To South Entrance

Legend:

- ▲ Campground
- 🍴 Food service
- 🛏 Lodging
- ⛽ Gas station
- Picnic area
- Ranger station
- Store
- Post Office
- Self-guiding trail
- Marina
- ⊕ Hospital

Inset scale: 0   0.25   0.5   Miles

*E*xploring the small, concentrated thermal region known as West Thumb Geyser Basin is a delight. Be sure to see the deep blue or, depending on water temperature, emerald-green waters of Abyss Pool, as well as lovely Bluebell Pool. These features are highlighted in the self-guiding trail leaflet available at the trailhead.

If you need more information or would like to purchase educational maps, books, and videos, visit the Yellowstone Association bookstore in the historic West Thumb Information Station, located next to the parking lot to the right (east) of the main highway, about 17 miles south of Old Faithful. In the summer this is also the meeting place for a variety of interpretive walks and talks.

The Grand Loop from West Thumb to Fishing Bridge is your chance to get to know one of the largest—more than 136 square miles, with more than 100 miles of shoreline—and most beautiful bodies of water in all the Rockies: Yellowstone Lake. Adding grandeur is the mighty Absaroka Range, scraping the sky far to the east. Yellowstone Lake rests atop the eastern edge of the Yellowstone Caldera, a mammoth depression formed by the collapse of ground after an enormous volcanic eruption some 650,000 years ago. Water eventually filled a portion of the depression, in some places to a depth of more than 300 feet, creating Yellowstone Lake.

Roughly 15 miles north of West Thumb, in the shadows of a beautiful climax forest of spruce and Douglas-fir, Gull Point Drive leaves the Grand Loop to wind along the lake's edge, offering numerous opportunities for picnics and lazy walks along the shore.

Several miles beyond Gull Point Drive is the turnoff to Bridge Bay Marina. Here, there are hour-long scenic boat rides around Stevenson Island, with interpretive guide services available. This is also the place to rent fishing gear, non-motorized boats, and small powerboats with crew and guide.

If you want to try your hand at fishing in Yellowstone, you can pick up the necessary permit, along with catch guidelines, at ranger stations, visitor centers, and general stores throughout the park. You may also want to check out the excellent exhibits on lake ecology, located at the visitor contact station near the marina.

West Thumb Geyser Basin was the first feature in Yellowstone to be described in a publication. A trapper named Daniel Potts wrote a letter to his brother in Pennsylvania, describing the thermal features. In 1827 the letter was printed in the Philadelphia Gazette. *It would be another forty-four years before the first scientific expedition visited West Thumb.* JEFF AND ALEXA HENRY

While winds can whip Yellowstone Lake into a frenzy at a moment's notice, those fortunate enough to see it in quiet times will never forget the sight. Clearly, this is not only one of the world's largest natural freshwater lakes, but one of the most beautiful. JEFF FOOTT

About 18 miles north of West Thumb on the Grand Loop Road, a turnoff to the right leads to Lake Village, where you will find a store, hospital, ranger station, Lake Lodge, and the beautiful Lake Hotel. Even if you are not staying at the hotel, it is definitely worth a closer look. Yellowstone's oldest hotel, Lake Hotel first opened its doors in 1891. The hotel had fallen into a state of disrepair by the 1970s, and in 1981 the National Park Service and park concessionaire TW Services (now Amfac Parks and Resorts) launched a ten-year renovation program to return the hotel to the glamorous look of its glory days of the early 1900s. ☙

Facing page: The Fishing Cone, on the shore of Yellowstone Lake in the West Thumb Geyser Basin. The first known use of Fishing Cone to actually cook fish occurred by accident in 1870, when a member of the Washburn Expedition accidentally dropped a trout off his line into the cone. When he retrieved it, it had been cooked. By the turn of the century, it seemed that every visitor to Yellowstone was determined to try it; this practice is now illegal. JEFF AND ALEXA HENRY

OVERWHELMED BY LAKE TROUT

If there's one ecology lesson we seem to need constant reminding of, it's this: You cannot pull one thread in the great web of life that makes up an ecosystem without disrupting the connecting strands. Take the case of lake trout, which are thought to have been illegally introduced into Yellowstone Lake. Unfortunately, lake trout now pose an extremely serious threat to native populations of cutthroat trout. As juveniles, lake trout compete fiercely with cutthroat for limited food resources; as adults they prey heavily on them. If left unchecked, lake trout could virtually wipe out the native cutthroat population.

As for the other strands in this web of life: Grizzly bears and other mammals are extremely dependent on spawning cutthroat, not to mention the many birds that feed on cutthroat during breeding season. Lake trout cannot replace cutthroat as a food source for these creatures. Lake trout breed in deep water during late fall, completely out of reach of predators, and, as adults, live in deeper waters than cutthroat, making them unavailable to virtually every bird except perhaps the deep-diving cormorant. Even anglers will probably not benefit, since most do not have the equipment needed to catch them.

Scientists are working hard on this problem: studying what lake trout eat and trying to figure out how to interrupt spawning activity. It is an extraordinary uphill battle, with success still out of sight. ∎

Lake trout.   ILLUSTRATION BY PETER GROSSHAUSER.

West Thumb to Fishing Bridge

WALKS AND HIKES

WEST THUMB GEYSER BASIN SELF-GUIDING TRAIL

Distance: The outer boardwalk loop is 0.5 mile long, while the inner loop is about 0.25 mile.

Difficulty: Easy.

Starting Point: The self-guiding boardwalks through the West Thumb Geyser Basin begin just east of the junction between the Grand Loop Road and the South Entrance Road, beside the Yellowstone Association bookstore in the historic ranger station.

Special Note: The walkways are wheelchair accessible, though assistance may be required between Twin Geysers and the junction of the middle and outer loops.

This trail will take you through the largest geyser basin on the shore of Yellowstone Lake. The magma chamber that heats Yellowstone's thermal features is especially close at hand here—less than 2 miles under the Earth's surface. The same thermal features found along these boardwalks do not end at the shore, but are found under the lake as well. In winter, when most of the lake is covered with 3 feet of ice, heat from underwater thermal features produces small pockets of open water.

The shorter, inner boardwalk trail leads past a series of intriguing springs: Surging Spring (which overflows into the lake), colorful Ledge Spring, Collapsing Pool, and Ephedra and Blue Funnel Springs. The outer boardwalk offers a close-up look at Abyss Pool, which at 53 feet is one of the deepest hot springs in the park, as well as Fishing Cone, located along the shore of Yellowstone Lake. Fishing Cone

gave rise to the bizarre practice—first by mountain men, later by tourists—of hooking trout and then whipping the rod around to cook them in this pool of boiling water. Alas, injuries to excited anglers prompted the closure of the site to all fishing.

ELEPHANT BACK

Distance: 4 miles round trip.

Difficulty: Easy to moderate (rises 800 feet in elevation in 0.8 mile).

Starting Point: On the left (north) side of the Grand Loop Road, 19 miles north of West Thumb.

This pathway begins in a lovely mature forest of Engelmann spruce, subalpine fir and lodgepole pine, with a floor peppered with whortleberry, common juniper, and Oregon grape. In about a mile the trail forks; stay left and follow the path to a splendid view of Yellowstone Lake to the south, and the beautiful Pelican Valley to the east. Continue around the loop to return.

A wild, glorious view of Yellowstone Lake from atop Elephant Back. The rugged peaks behind the lake are part of the Absaroka Range; in this area they rise to heights of more than 10,000 feet above sea level. MICHAEL SAMPLE

Fishing Bridge to Canyon Village

• Driving Time: 40 minutes • Distance: 16 miles

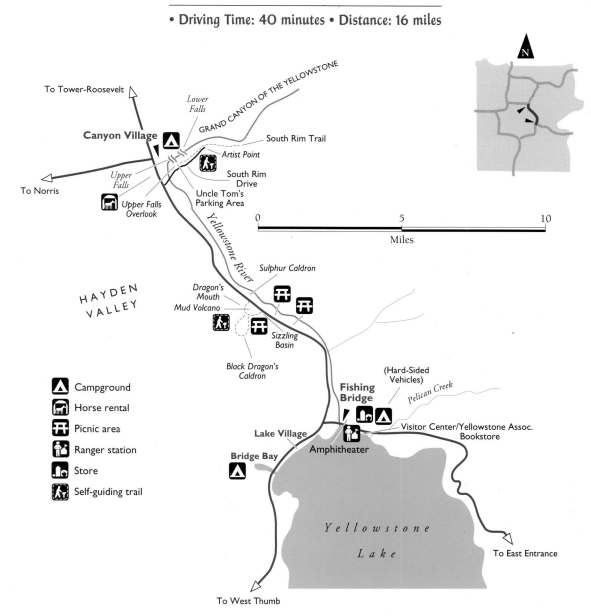

Campground

Horse rental

Picnic area

Ranger station

Store

Self-guiding trail

*I*f you are a lover of wildlife, take an early morning or late evening drive along the slice of Grand Loop road heading north out of Fishing Bridge. For starters, you will have the Yellowstone River for company, its cool, grassy banks playing host to hungry moose, elk, and deer.

On the left (west) side of the road, about 6 miles from Fishing Bridge, is the parking area for Mud Volcano. At Mud Volcano hot vapors escape from the earth through steam vents. These vapors, rich in sulfuric acid, break down the surrounding rock, making clay. Because there is not enough

water to wash away the acid or the leached rock, it is left as a pool of sticky mud. In the late 1800s this feature was extremely active, spewing out enough mud from a 30-foot cone to cover tall trees standing nearby.

Just a little farther up the highway on the right (east) is a turnout from which you can view Sulphur Caldron. This feature lives up to its name, complete with turbulent, splashing waters, yellow from the high sulphur content. This is among the most acidic springs in the entire park, about as sour as battery acid.

Beyond Sulphur Caldron, you are treated to the fantastic sweeps of Hayden Valley. Long ago Hayden Valley was filled by an arm of Yellowstone Lake. The clay, silt, and sand sediments from the lake, now covered by glacial debris, make for poor drainage in the bottom of the valley, which is why so much of this valley is covered with wet, swampy areas. Hayden Valley, one of the world's outstanding wildlife viewing areas, is home to bison, grizzly, elk, deer, and moose. In the river and along many of those wet areas, look for trumpeter swans, teal, goldeneyes, Canada geese, pelicans, fish-hunting bald eagles and osprey, and finally, that remarkably graceful, almost mystical-looking bird, the great blue heron.

The Yellowstone River exits the valley and heads north, and, forced into a narrower rocky waterway, it gathers momentum, turning, in the space of just a few miles, from a peaceful waterway to a thundering giant, strong enough to carve out the magnificent Grand Canyon of the Yellowstone River.

The great sweeps of the Hayden Valley remain some of the best places in Yellowstone to observe wildlife, especially bison. Out of the millions of bison that once roamed the country, by 1900 only one wild herd remained in the United States, in Yellowstone National Park. Today, Yellowstone's bison number roughly 1,600.
MICHAEL SAMPLE

Despite the name Fishing Bridge, angling has been prohibited here since 1973 as part of an effort to protect declining populations of cutthroat trout in Yellowstone Lake. However, it remains a wonderful place to observe trout. JEFF AND ALEXA HENRY

About 13 miles north of Fishing Bridge, on the right (east) side of the road, is South Rim Drive. This drive offers wonderful overlooks of the Yellowstone River as it roars through a magnificent volcanic canyon, cutting ever deeper into the soft rhyolite rock. The Upper Falls Overlook, reached by a path just west of Uncle Tom's Parking Area, offers a good view of the 109-foot Upper Falls. (Uncle Tom was Tom Richardson, one of the area's first concessionaires. He routinely guided people into the canyon, using rope ladders to get to the bottom!) The 308-foot Lower Falls can be seen via a trail that begins at the end of South Rim Drive, at Artist Point. ◑

BE ALERT FOR BEARS

Many trails around Yellowstone Lake and between Fishing Bridge and Canyon Village travel through prime grizzly bear habitat. At times overnight camping may not be allowed, and if bears have been recently spotted, certain trail segments may be closed. Before hiking off the self-guiding trails, you may wish to check at an area ranger station or visitor center for reports of bear activity. ▪▪

The Yellowstone River in a quiet mood, flowing through the Hayden Valley. The Yellowstone, at 671 miles in length, remains the last major river in the continental United States that has not been dammed.   MICHAEL SAMPLE

Fishing Bridge to Canyon Village

WALKS AND HIKES

MUD VOLCANO SELF-GUIDING TRAIL

Distance: 0.7 mile round trip.

Difficulty: Easy.

Starting Point: 6 miles north of Fishing Bridge.

Special Note: The ground surrounding the Mud Volcano Trail is extremely thin and fragile; stay on boardwalks to avoid serious injury from scalding.

Early Yellowstone exploration parties talked of being able to hear Mud Volcano a mile away and watching it toss great globs of mud far beyond its crater. Though it's settled down considerably since then, Mud Volcano remains an intriguing place.   MICHAEL SAMPLE

59

The face of this area, changed dramatically by earthquakes in 1978, is about as close to a sorcerer's collection of stew pots as you will find. Here are the dark, oozing mixture of Black Dragon's Caldron, the hiss of Sizzling Basin, and the thin, hot surge of water that rises and falls from the Dragon's Mouth.

ARTIST POINT SELF-GUIDING TRAIL

Distance: 0.25 mile round trip.

Difficulty: Easy.

Starting Point: Turn right off the Grand Loop Road, about 13 miles north of Fishing Bridge, onto South Rim Drive. Follow this for roughly 2 miles, to the end of the road.

This easy walk takes you to what some call the Grand Canyon of the Yellowstone River's most famous view spot. Here you are afforded sweeping views of 308-foot-high Lower Falls. Note the beautiful green stripe in the water that forms the falls. This coloring is caused by a notch located at the top of the falls, which allows a deeper, less turbulent stream of water to pass over the lip of the falls, making it appear more green than the water around it.

SOUTH RIM SELF-GUIDING TRAIL

Distance: 6.5 miles round trip.

Difficulty: Moderate.

Starting Point: 13 miles north of Fishing Bridge, turn right (east) onto South Rim Drive. Park in the lot on the far side of the bridge that crosses the Yellowstone River.

This trail, paved in places, winds along the south rim of the canyon and offers great views of the Lower Falls. In roughly 2 miles, the trail passes through the Artist Point parking area and continues beyond the parking area another 1.25 miles.

The thunderous Lower Falls of the Yellowstone—the highest of any waterfall in the park—has been inspiring visitors for well over a century. Early explorers seemed nearly overcome by the sight. One member of the Washburn exploring party of 1870 called this "the grandest waterfall in the world, surely destined to become a shrine for a world-wide pilgrimage." CAROL POLICH

An adult grizzly bear beside a clump of rose hips. The long claws of the grizzly bear, along with its tremendously powerful shoulder muscles, help it dig for roots and bulbs, as well as for ground-dwelling rodents and their caches of seeds and nuts. ERWIN AND PEGGY BAUER

WILDLIFE WATCHING

In the introduction to this guide we mentioned how important it is for visitors to interact safely with Yellowstone's rich variety of wild animals. One of the things that makes wild animals wild is that they have no bond with humans, no regular relationship. Even when you are at a safe distance, many animals will be extremely wary. Many animals give unmistakable signs when they are agitated; the problem is most of us no longer speak their language. When people continue to push the boundaries of a wild animal's comfort zone, its reaction is very unpredictable. Some animals will run. Others will stand their ground in a defensive posture. Still others will attack. Please remember that getting closer than 25 yards to all animals but bears (see below) is against the law. Getting too close will compromise your safety and will always result in added stress to the animals.

A special note about bears: Never get within 100 yards of a bear. Hikers can lessen the danger of a sudden encounter (the cause of most bear-related injuries to humans) by making noise as they walk, especially in areas where vision is restricted. Avoid animal carcasses and do not hike after dark. If you encounter a bear, do not run, since bears are fast sprinters. If the bear is unaware of your presence, detour away from the animal; if it sees you but does not act aggressively, slowly back away. If you are attacked, many experts advise playing dead. Drop to the ground, lift your legs to your chest, and clasp your hands over the back of your neck.

Remember, odors attract bears. Keep a clean camp and hang all food and odorous items (such as soap and deodorant) as far from your sleeping area as possible and at least 10 feet above the ground and 4 feet out from tree trunks. Or stow such items in a car or car trunk. If you have a conflict with a bear, report it to a park ranger as soon as possible. ▦

BISON

For many, the bison is the classic symbol of the American West. Indeed, millions of bison that once roamed the yawning, grassy prairies beyond Yellowstone were the staff of life for native cultures that flourished there, providing food, shelter, and clothing. Bison can weigh in at a whopping 2,000 pounds and are the largest animals you will see in Yellowstone.

Today, controversy surrounds Yellowstone's bison. Bison can and do carry a bacterial disease called brucellosis. Some believe that brucellosis, first detected in the park's bison in 1917, can be transmitted to livestock, causing domestic cows to abort their first calf. Researchers continue to try to develop effective vaccines. Meanwhile, there have been aggressive campaigns to control bison wandering out of the park onto neighboring cattle range; these include herding bison back into the park or destroying them.

Remember: Bison are dangerous. They injure or kill visitors every year. Enjoy them from a safe distance. ▦

Hayden Valley bison feeding along the Yellowstone River. While bull bison spend most of their year alone or in small groups, in late July and August they rejoin the herds for the rut. At that time the Hayden Valley is filled with the sights and sounds of bulls competing with each other for cows. MICHAEL SAMPLE

Canyon Village to Tower-Roosevelt

• Driving Time: 45 minutes • Distance: 19 miles

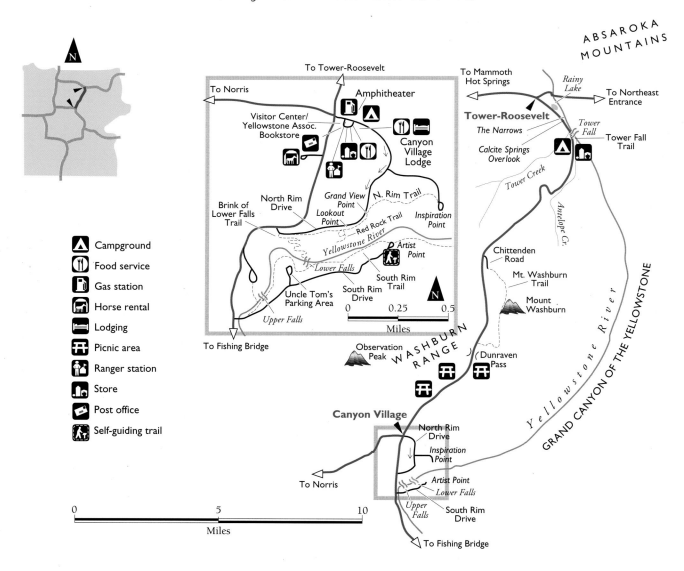

Key
- ▲ Campground
- 🍴 Food service
- ⛽ Gas station
- 🐴 Horse rental
- 🛏 Lodging
- 🏕 Picnic area
- 👫 Ranger station
- 🏪 Store
- ✉ Post office
- 🚶 Self-guiding trail

*F*rom Canyon Village, you can travel north to Tower-Roosevelt or west to Norris (next section). If you are coming from Fishing Bridge, turn right at the Canyon Village intersection and then right again into the parking lot for the visitor center. Park interpretive staff in the visitor center can help with your questions about the area; you may also wish to visit the Yellowstone Association bookstore. Beginning in mid-1997, the Canyon Visitor Center will host an engaging exhibit on bison, including several mounted specimens.

Of all the memories you will carry back with you from this magic place, few will be more satisfying than those of

the 23-mile-long Grand Canyon of the Yellowstone. This incredible chasm is best enjoyed via two roads off the Grand Loop: The North Rim Drive, a one-way road heading east from the crossroads at Canyon Village; and the South Rim Drive, heading right (east) from the Grand Loop Road, 3 miles south of the crossroads at Canyon Village.

Facing page: The brink of the Upper Falls of the Yellowstone, reached by way of a 0.25-mile, round-trip trail that takes off from North Rim Drive. Because the canyon bends between Upper and Lower Falls, there is no place to see both waterfalls at the same time.

JEFF FOOTT

The rugged Grand Canyon of the Yellowstone is a masterwork of erosion. In its entire 23-mile length there is only one trail reaching the bottom, this via a long and very strenuous route.
MICHAEL SAMPLE

In violent eruptions 650,000 years ago—when the magma chamber underlying this region erupted, collapsing the ground above it—debris spread across thousands of square miles. Water cutting through layers of this volcanic rock formed the Grand Canyon of the Yellowstone. Later, the chasm was excavated further by three different glaciers. Each of those glaciers plugged the neck of the canyon like a dam, allowing it to fill with water. When the ice melted, the canyon was flooded with raging torrents of meltwater loaded with abrasive sand and gravel.

Both the North Rim and South Rim Drives afford fine views of the Upper Falls and the larger, more dramatic Lower Falls. Like the canyon itself, both waterfalls owe their existence to erosion; each one formed where relatively hard lava rock joins softer material. As you might expect, water cuts through soft rock faster than it cuts through hard rock. In time, the softer section ends up lower than the more erosion-resistant stretch adjacent to it. Where hard and soft rock meet, a waterfall is formed. Besides the falls, another canyon wonder you cannot miss, whether on the North Rim Drive or the South Rim Drive, is the array of beautiful colors: gold, yellow, pink, and rust. Each is the result of hot water, steam, and gasses burnishing the rhyolite walls.

Once you have thoroughly explored the canyon, continue north on the Grand Loop Road toward Tower-Roosevelt. The road between Canyon Village and Tower-Roosevelt crosses some of the highest terrain accessible by road in Yellowstone and is usually closed until early June because of snowfall. Those driving or towing large RVs may wish to avoid this section as the twisting, two-lane road is narrow, with very steep roadside drop-offs and without guard rails in some sections. Soon after leaving Canyon Village, the road climbs the east flank of the Washburn Range toward 8,859-foot Dunraven Pass. Visible to the east is mighty Mount Washburn, its 10,243-foot peak capped by a fire lookout.

As you make your way down the north side of Dunraven Pass, the landscape turns into a loosely woven patchwork of aspen and Douglas-fir forest. Open meadows near Antelope Creek are filled with sage, geranium, wheatgrass, aster, lupine, and paintbrush. Elk, bison, and even grizzlies, can be seen ambling through the open country. In the distance to the north and east are the mighty Absaroka mountains, a rugged line of peaks towering well above timberline.

Tower Fall is located on the right (east) side of the Grand Loop Road, about 16 miles north of Canyon Village. Adjacent to the General Store is a short trail that will take you to a fine view of the falls, which tumble 132 feet out of a fantasy land of tower-shaped volcanic rock before joining forces with the Yellowstone River. As you leave the parking area to turn right toward Tower-Roosevelt, note the striking bands of color in the vertical basalt columns in the cliffs overhanging the road. These columns were formed by a lava flow that cracked into hexagon-shaped pillars as it cooled. Calcite Springs Overlook, about 1 mile ahead on your right, gives a bird's-eye view of the Narrows, the narrowest section of the Grand Canyon of the Yellowstone River. Farther up the road, 18 miles from Canyon Village, is a small, restful-looking body of water on the right, known as Rainy Lake. The lake takes its name from numerous small springs which bubble up and disturb the surface, making it appear as though it is raining. Just after Rainy Lake, you will arrive at Tower-Roosevelt. ☺

Depending on the light and the weather, the Grand Canyon of the Yellowstone can take on a variety of moods. Much of the beautiful color here is caused by the oxidation of iron in the rocks. MICHAEL SAMPLE

YELLOWSTONE

CANYON RIM TRAILS

An abundance of walkways and trails offer striking views into the wonders of the Grand Canyon of the Yellowstone. Before you lace up your hiking shoes, however, keep these important points in mind:

- Bears are frequent visitors to the canyon area. Before you explore the area, you may wish to check on the current bear situation by stopping at the visitor center.

- Several trails make steep descents into the canyon. These hikes are not recommended for people with heart, lung, or other health conditions.

- Many canyon trails are closed throughout the winter, as well as during unfavorable spring and fall conditions. Before you hike, check at the visitor center for current conditions.

- This is an area of steep, dangerous terrain, much of it at elevations of 8,000 feet or higher. Keep to the trails, and

As is true throughout Yellowstone, sights at the canyon are a mix of overwhelming grandeur and small, quiet marvels like this pine tree, perched on solid rock at the absolute edge of oblivion.
MICHAEL SAMPLE

stay behind the safety barriers at overlooks. Be especially careful in wet conditions. Do not throw objects into the canyon, as these could injure someone below. ▪▪

Canyon Village to Tower-Roosevelt

WALKS AND HIKES

INSPIRATION POINT SELF-GUIDING TRAIL

Distance: 0.2 mile round trip.

Difficulty: Moderate.

Starting Point: From the crossroads at Canyon Village, head east on one-way North Rim Drive. Follow this for just under 1 mile and turn left toward Inspiration Point. Follow this for 0.75 mile, to the end of the road. Parking is limited here for wide or long vehicles, however.

This trail leads down over some fifty steps to stunning views of the canyon. If you would like to hike farther, gaining

still more glimpses of the canyon, plan to follow the North Rim Trail, which begins in this same parking area, heading upstream (west) along the canyon rim. It is 3 miles on the North Rim Trail from Inspiration Point to the South Rim Drive Bridge.

GRAND VIEW SELF-GUIDING TRAIL

Distance: 0.2 mile round trip.

Difficulty: Easy.

Starting Point: From the crossroads at Canyon Village, head right (east) on one-way North Rim Drive. Follow this for about 1.25 miles to the pullout for Grand View, on your left.

This easy walk, especially beautiful in early morning hours, is the best view of the canyon's stunning colors on the North Rim. You may see steam vents near the river.

An adult bighorn ram surveys Yellowstone from a windswept summit. While bighorn feed on mountain herbs and grasses, there is always at least one member of the band keeping watch. At the slightest hint of danger, the entire group will run off to safety behind their leader. MICHAEL SAMPLE

RED ROCK SELF-GUIDING TRAIL

Distance: 0.75 round trip.

Difficulty: Difficult (500-foot elevation change).

Starting Point: From the crossroads at Canyon Village, head right (east) on one-way North Rim Drive. Follow this for slightly more than 1.5 miles to the pullout for Lookout Point, on your left. (NOTE: Those not physically able to hike down to Red Rock can still enjoy a fine view of Lower Falls from atop the rim, at Lookout Point, an excellent place to see ospreys, as well.)

This paved trail descends 500 feet over approximately one-third of a mile to a wonderful view of Lower Falls. At 308 feet high, this waterfall is twice as tall as Niagara Falls. Runoff varies from more than 60,000 gallons per second at peak season (typically occuring in June), to some 5,000 gallons per second in September and October.

MOUNT WASHBURN TRAILS

Distance: 6 miles round trip, leaving from the Dunraven Pass Picnic Area; 6 miles round trip, leaving from Chittenden Road. (Those with a shuttle car can start at Dunraven Pass and end at Chittenden.)

Difficulty: Difficult.

Starting Point: There are two trailhead options. The first is at Dunraven Pass Picnic Area (not Dunraven Picnic Area), located about 5 miles north of Canyon Village, on the right (east) side of the road. For the second trailhead, go north from Canyon Village 10 miles to Chittenden Road, and turn right. Follow this for about 1 mile to the parking area.

This 10,243-foot-high lookout offers glorious views. In summer, bighorn sheep frequent the flanks of Mount Washburn, having migrated here from the lowlands, and are often spotted feeding near the trails. (Enjoy them to your heart's content, but again, please do not feed or approach these or any other Yellowstone wildlife.) This area is also a good place to get a better view of whitebark pine, a tenacious, five-needled evergreen, with cones that during some years (depending on the crop) provide an important source of food for grizzlies.

TOWER FALL

Distance: 1 mile round trip.

Difficulty: Moderate (300 foot elevation change).

Starting Point: Beside the Tower Fall General Store.

Your first look at beautiful Tower Fall—so named for the volcanic spires surrounding the head of the fall—comes less than 100 yards from the parking lot. The view gets better as you make your way down to the base of the drop on a series of steep switchbacks.

The eroded volcanic pinnacles at the top of this 132-foot plunge make it easy to understand how Tower Fall got its name. During the late nineteenth century, Thomas Moran and Albert Bierstadt, well-loved landscape artists, created magnificent paintings of Tower Fall which played a big role in rallying public support for making Yellowstone a national park. MICHAEL SAMPLE

WHERE ARE THE BEARS?

Those who visited Yellowstone many years ago will recall the common sight of bears begging for food in developed areas, even feeding in open garbage dumps. Over time many bears not only became used to human food, they grew increasingly bold in their efforts to find it. The dumps were finally closed in the late 1960s, bearproof garbage containers were installed, and an educational campaign was launched to keep people from feeding the bears. As a result, both grizzly and black bears have returned to their natural feeding habits, well away from roadsides, where they are not easily seen. ▪

Of all of Yellowstone's creatures, few have captured the imagination of visitors like the magnificent grizzly bear. While grizzlies can be dangerous, especially when surprised, most avoid encounters with humans.   ERWIN AND PEGGY BAUER

Canyon Village to Norris

• Driving Time: 20 minutes • Distance: 12 miles

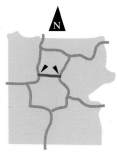

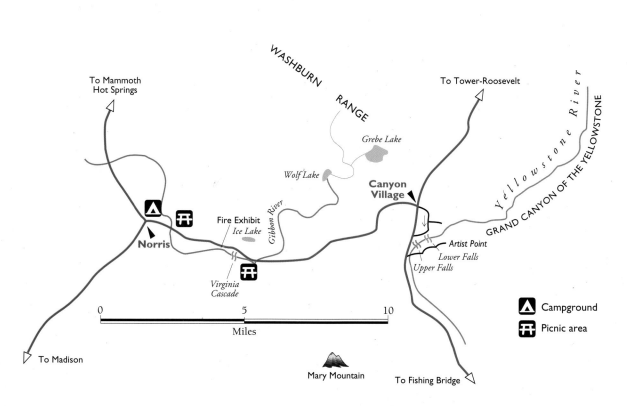

To Mammoth Hot Springs

WASHBURN RANGE

Grebe Lake

Wolf Lake

Gibbon River

Fire Exhibit
Ice Lake

Norris

Virginia Cascade

Canyon Village

To Tower-Roosevelt

Yellowstone River

GRAND CANYON OF THE YELLOWSTONE

Artist Point
Lower Falls
Upper Falls

| 0 | | 5 | | 10 |

Miles

To Madison

Mary Mountain

To Fishing Bridge

▲ Campground

⌗ Picnic area

As you make your way west across this 12-mile segment of the Grand Loop toward Norris, be sure to make a stop at the Fire Exhibit. This exhibit is located about 9 miles west of Canyon Village, on the left (south) side of the highway. An observation platform at the end of a short boardwalk offers a good glimpse into one of the hotter burns of the fires of 1988. While certain kinds of ground plants were flourishing in other areas soon after the 1988 burn, here the fire fed on an enormous jumble of dead timber, toppled by a massive wind storm four years earlier. As a result, the ground became so hot that many seeds and roots lying underground, which normally would be protected, were destroyed. This deep burn has made regeneration a slow process. Even so, clusters of lodgepole—a tenacious tree quick to reclaim burned ground—can be seen scattered across the area.

From here, the road makes a gentle pass across a high, forested plateau, much of it pocked with small ponds.

Near the end of this stretch, the road descends sharply into the Norris Geyser Basin area. Be particularly careful on this hill in late spring and early fall when snowfall can make the road slippery. ☙

Forest fires have been a critical part of the lifecycle in Yellowstone for at least 12,000 years. Fires help limit disease in trees, and they also thin crowded stands of timber, which in turn provides more grass for grazing wildlife. JEFF AND ALEXA HENRY

No one who fought fires in Yellowstone during the summer of 1988 will ever forget the experience. This was the largest fire suppression effort ever undertaken in the United States. The peak of the operation saw more than 9,000 firefighters, including several units from both the Army and the Marines. JEFF AND ALEXA HENRY

THE FIRES OF 1988

Spring of 1988 began like so many other springs in Yellowstone. Rain and snow fell in abundance. In fact, during April and May, precipitation came in amounts well above average. Not long afterward, however, the skies turned dry. June, July, and then August, came and went with almost no moisture—the driest summer ever recorded.

Regular forest fires had been burning through the Rockies for countless centuries. For a long time resource managers did not realize fires were serving an important function—removing jumbles of dead and fallen trees (part of the so-called "fuel load"). Fires helped eliminate diseased timber, at the same time creating an abundance of new grazing areas for wildlife. Fire was so long a part of the scene that some species, including the lodge-pole pine, actually evolved to thrive in the face of periodic burns. But in more modern times, managers vigorously suppressed every burn they could reach, aided greatly by the advent of airborne firefighting techniques. As a result, the fuel load increased to dangerous levels. In 1988 these levels, as well as remarkably high winds (sometimes pushing fire fronts 10 miles in a single day), lightning, and human carelessness (half of the 1988 fires were human-caused), came together to create the most extraordinary of fire seasons.

By summer's end, some 990,000 acres in Yellowstone Park had been touched by fire (roughly 45 percent of the park). However, only about one-quarter of those burns were severe enough to actually kill the trees and only a fraction of a percent were so hot they destroyed the seeds

and roots lying protected under the soil. In spite of massive human fire-fighting efforts, it took nature's moisture, coming as snow in early September, to finally end the fires of 1988.

In the wake of those burns, an abundance of new life is washing across these lands. Nutrient-rich mats of grasses and forbs have appeared, and acres and acres of young lodgepole crowd shoulder to shoulder in a race for the sun. Birds, insects, and small mammals find homes in burned trees. The cycle of life in Yellowstone continues as it has for thousands of years. ▦

Visitors to Yellowstone in the years following the 1988 fires have been treated to stunning displays of wildflowers. Fire actually plays an important role in returning nutrients to the soil. Studies in Yellowstone after the 1988 fires found that fireweed (the lavender flower) growing in burned areas was roughly 30 percent richer in nutrients than the same plant growing on unburned ground. JEFF FOOTT

Tower-Roosevelt to Mammoth Hot Springs

• Driving Time: 40 minutes • Distance: 18 miles

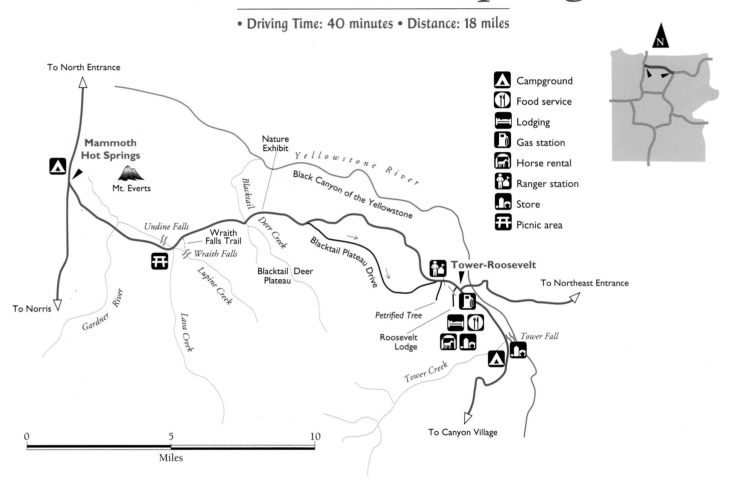

At Tower-Roosevelt you will find gas, phones, and a small ranger station (no exhibits). This is also the location of the historic Roosevelt Lodge, a popular guest facility built in 1920. Today, activities include trail and stagecoach rides, as well as Old West dinner cookouts.

The road between Tower-Roosevelt and Mammoth Hot Springs provides soaring views of the park's drier northern climate, which averages 40 to 50 percent less precipitation than areas farther south. (Annual precipitation in the park varies from a low of 14 inches at the north boundary to 38 inches in the southwest corner!) The smaller amount of moisture in this area contributes greatly to the beautiful landscape you will see along this drive: a loose patchwork of forests stitched into mile after mile of drifting, open valleys, and hillsides covered with sage, aster, and balsamroot.

Scattered around are large, solitary boulders, carried here thousands of years ago in the arms of glacial ice, then dropped in place as the climate warmed and the glaciers retreated. One-and-a-half miles from Tower-Roosevelt, on the left (south) side of the road, is the turnoff to Petrified Tree—a redwood tree that was buried in volcanic ash some 45 to 50 million years ago. For a tree to become petrified, it must be

Facing page: None of Yellowstone's large mammals is more plentiful than the elk; summertime populations are estimated at around 30,000 animals. Interestingly, the fires of 1988 created an unexpected additional source of winter food for elk. The bark of lodgepole pines, which elk normally cannot eat, went through chemical changes that transformed it into digestible food when burned. MICHAEL SAMPLE

buried quickly, minimizing decay. In addition, surrounding groundwater must have a high concentration of silica. Over time, silica-saturated water soaks into the tree, fills the spaces between the cells, and hardens.

Ten miles west of Tower-Roosevelt is a small, one-way dirt road heading onto Blacktail Deer Plateau, which eventually winds 7 miles back to rejoin the Grand Loop.

Beyond Blacktail Deer Drive, on the right, stop at a beautiful and fascinating exhibit (completion planned for 1999) that explains the natural processes and systems which shape Yellowstone. Plan to spend time here, as this exhibit summarizes much of what makes Yellowstone unique. This exhibit is an excellent example of the many wayside exhibits throughout Yellowstone for which the Yellowstone Association has provided significant funding.

Approximately 14 miles from Tower-Roosevelt (about 0.5 mile past the Lava Creek Picnic Area), on the right (north) side of the road, is the access to beautiful Undine Falls. This double waterfall, with a combined drop of more than 100 feet, was named for the mythological undine, a wise water spirit said to live around waterfalls.

Note the wild-looking, towering peaks that rise beyond the park to the north and northwest toward the Gallatin National Forest. The lands both inside and outside of the park are part of the northern elk range. This land of grass and sedges and various kinds of browse, of lowland valleys and cool uplands, supports the largest elk herd in Yellowstone, typically between 15,000 to 20,000 animals. Though variable, summer populations of elk in the park are estimated at about 30,000, giving Yellowstone the distinction of supporting the largest concentration of elk in the world. ⏺⏺

Tower-Roosevelt to Mammoth Hot Springs

WALKS AND HIKES

WRAITH FALLS

Distance: 1.8 miles round trip.

Difficulty: Easy.

Starting Point: Roughly 13 miles west of Tower-Roosevelt (0.5 mile east of the Lava Creek Picnic Area), on the left (south) side of the road.

Less than a mile of easy walking through sagebrush flats and coniferous forest brings you to the base of this comely falls—a stretch of Lupine Creek that tumbles about 100 feet in a braid of cold, white froth. The name Wraith, which refers to a spirit or specter, was given to this falls by a U.S. Geological Survey Party in 1885.

A Yellowstone *Field Guide*

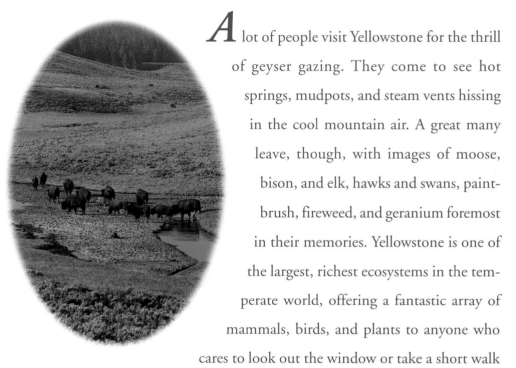

A lot of people visit Yellowstone for the thrill of geyser gazing. They come to see hot springs, mudpots, and steam vents hissing in the cool mountain air. A great many leave, though, with images of moose, bison, and elk, hawks and swans, paint-brush, fireweed, and geranium foremost in their memories. Yellowstone is one of the largest, richest ecosystems in the temperate world, offering a fantastic array of mammals, birds, and plants to anyone who cares to look out the window or take a short walk down a quiet pathway. The park has the largest concentration of large and small mammals in the lower 48 states, including 7 species of ungulates, more than 225 species of birds, and 18 species of fish.

There is one rule about wildlife watching that you must remember: Do not, under any circumstance, approach wildlife—no matter how tempted you may be, no matter who else may be doing it. When threatened, bison, elk, deer, moose, and bear have all struck out at humans, sometimes seriously injuring or killing them. Animals with young are particularly dangerous. If you truly care for the well-being of your family, and wish to avoid needlessly stressing the animals themselves, turn up the zoom on your video camera, but keep your distance at all times. Stay at least 25 yards from Yellowstone's large mammals and 100 yards from a bear. Needless to say, do not feed Yellowstone's animals. Human food can harm their digestive systems and, over time, makes wild animals less wary of dangers like cars or poachers.

Bison on summer range in the Hayden Valley. Note the rust-colored calf in the center of the group. Though bison calves continue to nurse throughout most of their first year, they're able to travel with the herd just one day after birth.

MICHAEL SAMPLE

MAMMALS

You can greatly improve your chances of seeing birds and mammals by following these simple guidelines:

a) Try to hide the outline of your figure by crouching behind rocks, trees, or vegetation, and if possible, avoid casting a shadow. Practice moving slowly, smoothly.

b) Remember, most animals can hear much better than we can. Walk carefully; avoid breaking twigs or rustling leaves. (Speaking of hearing, you can improve yours slightly by cupping your hands around the backs of your ears.) To avoid bears, however, remember the point is to make noise. That way, the bears will be aware of your presence and will probably avoid you. For more information about bear safety see page 61.

c) Most birds and animals can detect even small movements. Try to use your peripheral vision instead of turning your head.

d) Accomplished wildlife watchers look for shapes that seem out of place—something rounded on a tree branch, for example—as well as for sudden motions.

e) Wildlife watching can be especially good right after a rain; birds come out to feed on displaced insects, and carnivores often look for flooded-out rodents.

f) Photographers do best with at least a 400 mm lens, with the sun at their backs, and in late afternoon light.

g) Generally speaking, early morning (about dawn) and late evening (just before dusk) are the best times to see wildlife. ∂∂

BIGHORN SHEEP

In winter these magnificent animals can be found at lower elevations from Mount Everts to Mount Norris; in summer look for them along the trail to Mount Washburn, on Specimen Ridge, and throughout the high country in the northeast portion of the park. Population sizes are highly variable. In late fall, rams battle to establish rank, sometimes lunging at one another with a crack of horns that can be heard a mile away. The horns on a mature male will be fully curled, whereas the horns on females are much shorter, rather like those of a goat, and less thick at the base.

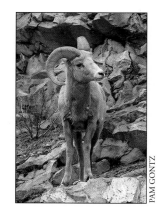
PAM GONTZ

BISON

Visitors in late July to mid-August stand a good chance of seeing the rut (breeding season), which is marked by bulls pushing and shoving each other for breeding privileges. Single calves are born in May and early June. Look for bison in Lamar Valley and Lower Geyser Basin, along the Madison River, and in Hayden Valley. Large numbers winter in Lamar Valley, in the Pelican Valley, and at Mary Mountain.

MICHAEL SAMPLE

PRONGHORN

Sometimes mistakenly called antelope, pronghorn are the fleetest of Yellowstone's animals, able to run for short distances at speeds of more than 60 miles per hour. In winter, pronghorn are found at low altitudes, especially in grassy areas below Mammoth Hot Springs; in spring, pronghorn migrate up the Yellowstone River to the Lamar Valley. They are rarely seen at high altitudes.

PAM GONTZ

ELK

A large mammal—bulls may reach 1,100 pounds—elk are tan colored with a dark brown head and neck and a buff-colored rump patch. Bulls begin to grow antlers in early spring, soon after shedding those from the previous year. Summer visitors will find these antlers covered in a soft skin, commonly known as velvet, which provides nourishment to the antlers as they grow. Besides being smaller, females do not have antlers. Bulls begin to "bugle" a high-pitched whistling sound in late August. Some biologists view bugling not as a challenge to rival bulls, but rather as an expression of the pent up stress and emotion that attend the mating season. Elk are seen in all habitats, but tend to be in high country mid-summer through fall, and then return to lowland valleys for the winter months.

MICHAEL SAMPLE

MOOSE

During summer this largest member of the deer family frequents marshy meadows and edges of lakes and streams. To keep from sinking in mud while feeding, as the animal lowers its foot, a large dewclaw spreads to better support the weight. Similarly, the odd-looking crook of the hind leg allows a moose to pull the leg straight up, more easily releasing it from deep, sucking mud. Male moose shed their antlers in spring, and shortly thereafter begin to grow new ones. For much of the summer, these antlers are covered in a soft, vascular skin, often referred to as velvet, which nourishes the antlers as they grow. Female moose do not have antlers. Take note—cow moose with young can be particularly dangerous.

MICHAEL SAMPLE

MULE DEER

The name comes from the deer's very large, mule-shaped ears. Not as numerous as elk; look for mule deer (also called Blacktail deer) in the park's open forests and meadows. Male deer, elk, and moose shed their antlers each year and grow new ones which are protected during growth by a soft covering called velvet.

MICHAEL SAMPLE

BLACK BEAR

It is estimated that there are from 500 to 600 black bears in Yellowstone. Like grizzlies, they are largely vegetarian, though most do not hesitate to feed on carcasses. Expect to see black bears in meadows during the summer months, or in forested areas with fruiting plants in the fall. The average weight of adult male black bears in Yellowstone is 210 to 315 pounds. Females weigh between 135 to 160 pounds. (See grizzly bear description for comparison.) Both black bears and grizzly bears range in color from almost buff to brown or black.

NATIONAL PARK SERVICE PHOTO

GRIZZLY BEAR

A grizzly bear can be distinguished from a black bear by the distinct hump on its back, as well as by a face that is somewhat "pushed in," or dished, between the forehead and nose. The long claws of the grizzly allow it to dig easily for roots and bulbs, rip apart logs for insects, and even excavate burrows for ground squirrels. Like black bears, grizzlies spend much of the winter sleeping; but they are not true hibernators, as their pulse and respiration remain nearly normal. Male grizzly bears in Yellowstone weigh from 216 to 717 pounds, while females range from 200 to 428 pounds.

STEVE TORREY

COYOTE

Coyotes can be seen throughout the park. Their survival is linked to a willingness to dine on a wide variety of foodstuffs, including mice, ground squirrels, voles, and other small mammals; bulbs,

MICHAEL SAMPLE

insects, and berries; as well as scavenging larger animals killed either by other predators, old age, or harsh winters. This habit of feeding on carcasses has sometimes resulted in serious conflicts with wolves that show little tolerance for coyotes scavenging their kills. Yellowstone coyotes are quite large and are often mistaken for wolves. (See wolf description for comparison.)

WOLF

The wolf is much heavier than the coyote (70 to 120 pounds, compared to 27 to 33 pounds) and longer in the leg. During warm months wolves tend to remain inactive during

NATIONAL PARK SERVICE PHOTO

the day; if you really want to see them, plan to do your watching at dawn. The Lamar Valley can be a good place to watch for these animals, especially from late fall through the end of June. Keep in mind most of Yellowstone's wolves feed primarily on elk; find the elk, and you stand a better chance of finding wolves.

YELLOWBELLIED MARMOT

The marmot is common throughout the park in summer, but a long hibernation season—mid-fall through April or May—leaves marmots unwatchable for much of the year. Most

PAM GONTZ

never stray very far from their dens, which are typically located within the protection of rock clefts or talus. On clear mornings look for them lying or standing on rocks, soaking up the sun. Marmots are frequently seen on the boardwalks around Old Faithful. Yellowbellied marmots are much bigger than ground squirrels; adults weigh in at 3.5 to more than 10 pounds, compared to just 7 to 10 ounces for the average Uinta ground squirrel.

UINTA GROUND SQUIRREL

Buff colored with black tail hairs that are lightly tipped, the Uinta ground squirrel is common in open, grassy areas amidst clumps of sagebrush. The Uinta ground squirrel prefers moist soil, which makes it especially plentiful near waterways, such as along the Madison River. The squirrels are often also seen on the lawn in front of the Mammoth Visitor Center. Other ground squirrels

PAM GONTZ

include the Richardson's, which has a smoky gray coat, and the golden-mantled, which looks rather like a large chipmunk. Please do not feed these or any other Yellowstone wildlife.

CHIPMUNK

Yellowstone's chipmunks are often seen in forested areas with fallen trees, which make useful runways for traveling back and forth from foraging areas. Where food is plentiful, look for

MICHAEL SAMPLE

chipmunks to make trip after trip, caching seeds for the winter ahead. The chipmunk's facial stripes distinguish it from a ground squirrel. No matter how these animals may try to "talk you into it," please do not feed them, or any other park wildlife.

BIRDS

*H*appily, many species of birds in Yellowstone today are success stories, having come back from zero or very low population levels just a few decades ago. Good examples are the trumpeter swan, osprey, bald eagle, and most recently, the peregrine falcon. When we talk about not approaching wildlife, we are talking about birds, too. Adult birds, especially ground nesters, will sometimes abandon their nest at the approach of humans, leaving the eggs or young exposed—not only to weather, but to hungry predators. ✍

CLARK'S NUTCRACKER

*T*his large, handsome bird, with a raspy voice that can be heard ringing throughout Yellowstone all year long, can be found from the lowest elevations to above timberline. This bird's habit of hanging from trees while hammering for grubs led Lewis and Clark to list it as a new species of woodpecker. Clark's nutcrackers are larger than gray jays and have heavier beaks.

ERWIN AND PEGGY BAUER

GRAY JAY

*T*his jay is a bold, gray-colored bird of the forest, about 10 inches long, with a raspy call. Gray jays have been called "camp robbers" for their habit of stealing food from campsites and picnic tables. It is important that you do not feed these birds. It is unlawful to do so, and human food can be unhealthy for them. Over time, handouts can leave these birds less able to thrive in the wild.

MICHAEL SAMPLE

MAGPIE

*T*he magpie is a most beautiful scavenger and thief, boasting a striking black and white coat with long black tail feathers. Sometimes the black appears as an iridescent green or blue color. These birds have a loud, raucous call, a rather nasal-sounding "mag!mag!" Magpies are common in certain local areas, from sagebrush meadows, to mixed forests, to willow-and-alder thickets near riparian zones.

MICHAEL SAMPLE

RAVEN

*R*avens are found in a wide variety of habitats all months of the year. Look for ravens on cliffs and talus slopes, in aspen and Douglas-fir forests, and on open reaches of grass and sage. These large, soaring birds, which will eat nearly anything, like to build their bulky nests on the cliff faces. Ravens are very assertive; do not feed them, and secure your food and valuables when they are nearby.

MICHAEL SAMPLE

OSPREY

This is a magnificent raptor nearly 2 feet long, with white underparts and a broad, black stripe passing through the eye and down either side of the neck. Living entirely on fish, the

MICHAEL SAMPLE

osprey is never far from lakes and rivers; the area around the Grand Canyon of the Yellowstone River is an especially good place to spot them.

CANADA GOOSE

These large birds with black heads and white cheeks have a distinct "honking" call, long considered one of the great sounds of the wilderness. Before migrating in fall, adult

MICHAEL SAMPLE

Canada geese molt their feathers, leaving them unable to fly for several weeks. Look for these wonderful birds along rivers and lakeshores throughout the park.

WHITE PELICAN

Pelicans nest in the park; look for them in Hayden Valley and at Yellowstone Lake, where they can sometimes be seen swimming abreast, pushing insects, fish, and crustaceans ahead of

ERWIN AND PEGGY BAUER

them and then scooping them into their pouches.

MOUNTAIN BLUEBIRD

Usually seen in aspen or coniferous forests, as well as in grasslands and meadows below timberline, males wear a stunning coat of sky blue feathers with a white belly, while females show blue only on the rump, tail, and wings. Mountain bluebirds feed on insects, and often nest in old woodpecker holes.

BALD EAGLE

Though bald eagles are found in a variety of habitats, they are often spotted along waterways. These birds are not common in the park except in winter, when you can find them

ERWIN AAND PEGGY BAUER

perched high in the trees of Lamar and Hayden Valleys. It takes four to five years for young eagles to acquire their distinctive white head feathers.

MALLARD

The striking, iridescent-green head (sometimes with a purplish cast) is the telling feature of this common duck, found in the park throughout the year. Look for mallards feeding in the shallow waters of Yellowstone's ponds, lakes, and rivers.

MICHAEL SAMPLE

TRUMPETER SWAN

This beautiful, snow-white bird with its straight neck and black beak, very nearly became extinct in the first half of the twentieth century; heroic restoration efforts made at Red Rock Lakes

MICHAEL SAMPLE

National Wildlife Refuge in extreme southwest Montana helped to bring the species back. Trumpeter swans nest in the park, but seem easiest to spot during autumn months. Look for them along the Madison River, in small kettle ponds along the Northeast Entrance Road east of Tower-Roosevelt, at Swan Lake, and in Hayden Valley.

PLANTS

*T*he climate of Yellowstone has changed dramatically from the subtropical conditions of 50 million years ago—the days of ferns, redwood, magnolia, and laurel. Today's conditions range from cool-temperate to subarctic, which translates into a mix of flowering plants that have very little time to bloom and set seed.

As you drive and walk through the park, take special note of the remarkable difference location can make: a south-facing slope will often support an entirely different vegetative mix than a north-facing slope; a couple of fallen Engelmann spruce can open up the woods for an entire garden of shrubs and flowers; and the dry, dark, acidic floor of lodgepole forest is much less hospitable than the floor of aspen woods.

Please remember: It is illegal to pick plants or flowers within the boundaries of the national park. ꙮ

ASPEN

PAM GONTZ

*A*spen is the most widely distributed tree in North America. It is sometimes called quaking aspen—a reference to the way its leaves flutter in the slightest breeze, because of a flattened leafstalk. The smooth, white bark of aspen can serve as a kind of wildlife ledger; here you will often find claw marks of black bears, or black scars at the base, showing how far hungry elk reached to peel and eat the bark on a cold winter day. In fall, aspen turn a bright golden-yellow.

ENGELMANN SPRUCE

MICHAEL SAMPLE

*T*his is a large, conical tree with beautiful dark needles. In this region, spruce sometimes reach heights of 75 feet. Engelmann spruce is one of the so-called climax trees; its seedlings are able to thrive in the shade of other trees. Barring wind and fire, this hardiness allows it to eventually "inherit" the woods. Common to higher elevations, generally above 8,400 feet, this tree can be found in the southwest and eastern uplands of the park, as well as in the Washburn Range.

DOUGLAS-FIR

GEORGE WUERTHNER

*T*his massive tree has a crown of slightly drooping branches and dark yellowish-green needles. When it comes to lumber, this is the most important timber species in America. In the right growing conditions, Douglas-fir can reach mammoth proportions. It is found in mixed forests at 6,500 to 7,500 feet, and is especially common in Lamar and Lower Yellowstone River Valleys, as well as in lower portions of the park's northwest corner.

LODGEPOLE PINE

JEFF HENRY

*O*ne of the most common trees—not just in Yellowstone, but throughout much of the Inter-mountain West—is named for its widespread use in Native American tipi building. Some of the cones of lodgepoles do not open except in the presence of fire; this allows new trees to get a quick start on burned ground. The lodgepole grows thickly across Yellowstone's central plateaus, at elevations of 7,600 to 8,400 feet.

BALSAMROOT

An early bloomer, this flower often colors dry hillsides in Yellowstone with a splendid wash of gold. In late spring you may see bighorn sheep feasting on both the leaves and flowers of this plant. This plant is most often seen in the northern reaches of the park.

PAM GONTZ

FIREWEED

Some say this plant is named for its prompt regrowth after fires. Others claim that its elongated reddish-purple flowers resemble flame. The plant's tiny seeds are strung with light, silky hairs that allow easy dispersal of the seeds by the wind. Fireweed is a nutritious source of food for both elk and grizzly bear. It is found in open sagebrush areas in the northern reaches of the park, as well as in burned forests.

PAM GONTZ

LUPINE

Look for the spikes of these blue and, rarely, white flowers throughout July and into August, both on open hillsides and in moist aspen and pine woods. If you are out watching elk, expect the animals to munch the flowers; grizzly and black bears, on the other hand, have a taste for the pods and roots.

MICHAEL SAMPLE

RABBITBRUSH

A bushy, 1-to 3-foot-tall plant, with branches and leaves covered with fine white hairs, rabbitbrush grows in the dry, poor soils of northern Yellowstone, often with sagebrush, and sports feathery-looking golden flowers in late summer and early fall. Elk rely on rabbitbrush for food throughout the winter months.

MICHAEL SAMPLE

YELLOW MONKEYFLOWER

Look for this perennial's bright yellow blooms along streams and in marshy areas from early June into August. The size of the plant, ranging from a couple of inches to nearly 2 feet, varies widely depending on elevation and soil quality.

GLENN VAN NIMWEGEN

FRINGED GENTIAN

Throughout the month of July and well into August, keep an eye on stream banks, wet meadows, and areas near warm springs for this plant's lovely lavender flowers. Fringed gentian is an annual, ranging from 4 to 16 inches tall. In 1926, it became Yellowstone National Park's official flower.

PAM GONTZ

PAINTBRUSH

One of the most striking splashes of color in all of Yellowstone, paintbrush make only a portion of their own food, securing the rest by penetrating the roots of other nearby plants such as sagebrush. Widely distributed in open areas and along roadsides throughout the park, paintbrush is Wyoming's state flower.

PAM GONTZ

SAGEBRUSH

A common plant of many open hillsides and valley floors throughout Yellowstone. Growing 1 to 5 feet tall, this is an important food source for pronghorn and mule deer especially in late winter and early spring.

MICHAEL SAMPLE

Conclusion

*I*t seems safe to say that even those who championed the creation of Yellowstone National Park in 1872 probably never imagined the real significance of their actions. The incomparable roar of geysers, the overwhelming bounty of wildlife, and the long, sweet roll of untrammeled landscapes are all gifts that have become increasingly precious in modern times. Held in this wellspring of diversity is the chance for all visitors to rediscover wildness, to savor a slice of unbound grandeur.

Increasingly, Yellowstone is serving not just the needs of spirit and recreation, but science as well. Its pool of genetic diversity is allowing a wealth of valuable new discoveries—micro-organisms found in Yellowstone's hot springs have become critical keys to unlocking the world of genetic "fingerprinting." The park is a land of opportunities for better understanding disease patterns in native fish and wildlife, and provides a baseline—a control group, if you will—with which we can better track everything from global climate changes to increases in air and water pollution.

As our ability to understand how natural systems work has increased, it has become readily apparent that Yellowstone cannot exist as an island; it is at the heart of an ecosystem that extends well beyond its borders. The majority of the park's famous elk herds, for instance, migrate out of Yellowstone each winter to feed in low-lying valleys on national forests and on private lands. Resource development that compromises water quality outside the park can also compromise fisheries and other life forms inside the park. Tapping into geothermal pools miles from the park could forever alter the delicate plumbing system that drives Yellowstone's geysers and hot springs. The solution doesn't depend on shutting down the ecosystem to all human activity. We must be willing to apply our best effort to understand how this ecosystem works, and to know it well enough to make intelligent choices about what should and should not happen outside the park.

Visit Yellowstone often. Adopt it as your own. Help in any way you can to make sure the world's first national park will always be a place that delights and amazes—that it will forever be here to teach us how to live well with the Earth. ❧

FOR MORE INFORMATION

National Park Service interpretive rangers are available to answer your questions at visitor centers, information stations, or museums at Mammoth Hot Springs, Old Faithful, Norris, Canyon Village, Fishing Bridge, Grant Village, Madison, and West Thumb. Your children may wish to participate in Yellowstone's Junior Ranger program during your visit; inquire at any of these locations.

Protecting Yellowstone and continuing to communicate its meaning to the world is vital to its preservation. The non-profit Yellowstone Association, in partnership with the National Park Service, fosters the public's understanding, appreciation, and enjoyment of Yellowstone National Park and its surrounding ecosystem by funding and providing educational products and services. In addition to operating Yellowstone Visitor Center bookstore sales areas (which make educational materials available to visitors), and using the proceeds for educational exhibits and programs in Yellowstone, the Yellowstone Association provides informative newsletters about Yellowstone to its national and international members. The Association also operates the Yellowstone Association Field Institute, an in-park field school offering a wide array of natural and cultural history classes. For more information about how you can join the Yellowstone Association, attend an Institute class, or make a donation to support critical educational and research projects, please call 307-344-2296 or write: Yellowstone Association, P.O. Box 117, Yellowstone National Park, WY 82190. http://www.YellowstoneAssociation.org ⊞